D1518151

FALSEHOOD
DISGUISED

volume 7

FALSEHOOD DISGUISED

Unmasking

the Truth in

La Rochefoucauld

Richard G. Hodgson

Purdue University Press
West Lafayette, Indiana

12-13-96 dmi

99   98   97   96   95   5   4   3   2   1

The paper used in this book meets the minimum requirements of
American National Standard for Information Sciences—Permanence of
Paper for Printed Library Materials, ANSI Z39.48-1984.

Printed in the United States of America
Design by Anita Noble

Library of Congress Cataloging-in-Publication Data
Hodgson, Richard G., 1950–
      Falsehood disguised : unmasking the truth in La Rochefoucauld /
Richard G. Hodgson.
            p.   cm. —(Purdue studies in Romance literatures ; v. 7)
      Includes bibliographical references and index.
      ISBN 1-55753-063-7 (alk. paper)
            1. La Rochefoucauld, François, duc de, 1613–1680. Maximes.
2. Truthfulness and falsehood in literature. 3. Maxims, French—
History and criticism. 4. Truth in literature. I. Title. II. Series.
PQ1815H63 1995
848'.402—dc20   94-38421
                                                                  CIP

For Debbie

Il y a des faussetés déguisées qui représentent si bien la vérité que ce serait mal juger que de ne s'y pas laisser tromper.

La Rochefoucauld, *Maxime* 282[†]

. . . *les* Maximes *sont à la longue comme un cauchemar de vérité.*

Roland Barthes, *Nouveaux essais critiques*[‡]

[†] There are disguised falsehoods which imitate the truth so well that it would be poor judgment not to let them deceive us.

[‡] . . . in the final analysis, the *Maximes* are like a nightmare of truth.

Contents

Portrait of La Rochefoucauld from the *Album* accompanying the Grands
Ecrivains de la France edition of his complete works (Paris: Hachette, 1883).

Preface

Like many of his seventeenth-century contemporaries, La Rochefoucauld was passionately interested in the nature of truth. He learned very early that given the powerful internal and external forces at work to prevent human beings from successfully carrying out their endless search for truth, distinguishing truth from falsehood in human affairs is neither easy nor self-evident. Throughout his life, La Rochefoucauld's close observation of those around him made him acutely aware that as human beings we all have extremely limited means at our disposal for discovering the truth, both about ourselves and about others. Analyzing the causes and consequences of this fundamental problem is one of La Rochefoucauld's primary concerns.

The principal objective of this study is to elucidate La Rochefoucauld's concept of truth. This idea will be examined through close textual analysis of both the *Maximes* and the *Réflexions diverses*. Although the *Maximes* have attracted considerable critical attention over the years, the *Réflexions diverses* have been thoroughly explored by only a few specialists, most recently by Jean Lafond. Modern criticism of La Rochefoucauld has focused on many issues, but no one has yet attempted to study his sometimes enigmatic pronouncements concerning truth and the extraordinary lengths to which human beings are willing to go to disguise truth from others and especially from themselves.

La Rochefoucauld's reflections on the problem of truth are centered on the idea of falsehood disguised, a concept which suggests that finding the truth in human affairs is difficult, largely because human beings will routinely do almost anything to conceal the falsity of their motives. Since individuals wear many masks, their true identity remains hidden, even from themselves. Compounding the problem is the fact that there are countless other forces at work—inside and outside the human psyche—which prevent the *être vrai,* the genuine person within each individual, from dropping his or her disguise.

In addition to the textual exegesis that is the basis of this study, I present La Rochefoucauld's ideas in the context of the views of some of his predecessors (Montaigne, Gracián, and Dyke) and of his most prominent contemporaries (Pascal,

Descartes, and Nicole). In so doing, I have brought to light both the close affinities and the major differences that exist between the works of these other moralists and the writings of La Rochefoucauld. My goal has been to elucidate his ideas by contextualizing them.

The introduction presents the central issue to be addressed by setting forth La Rochefoucauld's general pronouncements on the concepts of truth and falsehood. In Chapter Two, the Baroque underpinnings of his worldview are examined. Chapter Three describes the *être vrai* and its relation to the metaphor of the mask. The next three chapters outline the connections between the concept of truth/falsehood and the related concepts of self-love, the passions, and vice and virtue. Chapters Seven and Eight delve into the social repercussions of La Rochefoucauld's views on truth/falsehood. The final two chapters trace the impact of La Rochefoucauld's ideas on some major thinkers since his time and suggest reasons why his work seems so modern to readers in the late twentieth century.

Acknowledgments

I would like to thank all the people who helped me, directly and indirectly, with the writing of this book. My warmest thanks go to my colleagues and friends Larry Bongie and Ralph Sarkonak, who read the manuscript with great care and provided much-needed criticism and suggestions. I would also like to thank Harold Knutson, who read an earlier version of the manuscript. Research assistants Susan Bree and Kathleen Elliott cheerfully spent long hours gathering material for this volume.

Over the years, many people have helped to spark and to sustain my interest in La Rochefoucauld. I would particularly like to thank Olivier Abrioux, whose enthusiasm for seventeenth-century French literature still inspires me, and former students Charlotte Jull, Denis Combet, and Ellen Brown, who share my enduring interest in the *moralistes*.

I would like to thank the anonymous readers of Purdue Studies in Romance Literatures, who made many useful suggestions on the style and the format of this book. I wish to thank the editors of the *Archiv für das Studium der neueren Sprachen und Literaturen* for permission to publish, as part of Chapter Two, a reworked version of my article "La Rochefoucauld and the Baroque Concept of *Inconstance*" (228.2 [1991]: 311–20).

My thanks also to Floyd St.-Clair and David Watmough, whose caring and encouragement helped me through my sabbatical, when most of this book was written, and to Barbara and David Lemon, for their interest in my work. I would like to express special thanks to my friend Jo-Ann McEachern, an *être vrai* whose practical advice and moral support have been invaluable to me.

Finally, I would like to express my thanks to Shabe Lohrasbe. And to my wife, Debbie, who has given me her love and support for more than two decades.

L'Amour de La Vérité

Frontispiece of the early editions of the *Maximes* (reprinted from the *Album* of the Grands Ecrivains de la France edition of the complete works).

Chapter One

Introduction

Truth and Falsehood in La Rochefoucauld

*La vérité ne fait pas tant de bien dans le monde
que ses apparences y font de mal.*
                    La Rochefoucauld, *Maxime* 64[†]

*Nous souhaitons la vérité, et ne trouvons en nous
qu'incertitude.*
                    Pascal, *Pensée* 20[‡]

The frontispiece of the 1665 edition of La Rochefoucauld's *Maximes* displays a Cupid-like winged figure who has just removed a mask from a bust of Seneca. The scene depicted has often been viewed as symbolizing La Rochefoucauld's attitude toward Stoicism in general and the classical concept of "virtue" in particular. However, because this mysterious figure is described as "L'Amour de la Vérité" ("The Love of Truth"), this undoubtedly symbolic act of unmasking can also be seen as emblematic of another, even more important issue which La Rochefoucauld raises throughout the *Maximes* and *Réflexions diverses:* the search for truth. Finding the truth and ultimately revealing it to others, according to La Rochefoucauld, always involves lifting the mask of falsehood that has hitherto partially or entirely obscured it from view.

There can be little doubt that this frontispiece symbolizes La Rochefoucauld's view of Seneca and, more specifically, his position regarding the concept of "la vertu de constance." In addition, it clearly embodies, in the context of the wise man's

---

[†] Truth does less good in the world than its appearances do harm.
[‡] We desire truth, and are dogged by uncertainty.

1

search for truth, the two ideas that La Rochefoucauld saw as key elements in that search: first, that truth is almost always hidden or disguised and, second, that the process of revealing it, to oneself or to others, requires the revealing of the many disguises falsehood can wear and which must be discovered and removed before truth can be found. In other words, truth can be unmasked successfully only after falsehood in one or more of its many forms has been identified and denounced as such. Although La Rochefoucauld rarely uses the term *mask,* his work is full of imagery that suggests veiling and unveiling, disguising and the dropping of disguises, the concealing from oneself as well as from others of the individual's innermost thoughts and true motivations. The more closely one studies La Rochefoucauld's work, the more one realizes that it is the twin concepts of falsehood disguised and of truth unmasked that underlie his view both of human nature ("man alone with himself," as Nietzsche put it) and of "man in society." It is not just when he is explicitly discussing the nature of truth and falsehood that these concepts tend to appear, but also when he is analyzing the multiple functions of self-love, theorizing about the passions, or describing the difficulties of distinguishing virtues from vices. Whether he is dissecting the "anatomy" of the human heart in order to study its inner workings or explaining the fragile foundations of social harmony, La Rochefoucauld constantly confronts the problems created by the innate predilection for falsifying true motives and for disguising that falsity while at the same time presenting them as true needs and desires. The lies and other illusions of human creation with which individuals must perpetually deal (both their own and those of others) would not pose such a serious problem, according to La Rochefoucauld, were it not for the constant and insatiable human need for truth.

If it is true, as Nietzsche contends in *Menschliches, Allzumenschliches (Human, All Too Human),* that the methodical search for truth is "das Resultat jener Zeiten, in denen die Ueberzeugungen mit einander in Fehde lagen" ("a product of those ages in which convictions were at war with one another"),[1] no better example of such an age could be found than the seventeenth century in France and no better supporting evidence cited than the *Maximes* and *Réflexions diverses* of La Rochefoucauld.[2]

As critics from Jean Lafond to Louis Van Delft have shown, La Rochefoucauld's writings (exclusive of his *Mémoires*) are a battleground on which various warring convictions, in the form of very different and even opposing religious, moral, and political ideas, meet, conflict, and even, in more than one instance, contradict one another. In the *Maximes* and even more dramatically in the *Réflexions,* Augustinian and Jansenist attitudes[3] confront morally subversive and nihilistic ideas most often associated with the work of the *libertins érudits.* In a similar way, what Van Delft has called "la culture mondaine"[4] informs La Rochefoucauld's moral ideas just as much as does his aristocratic background or his reading of Aristotle.

It can reasonably be argued that the confluence in the work of La Rochefoucauld of these important currents in seventeenth-century French intellectual history goes a long way toward explaining the moralist's passionate search for truth. He lived, after all, in a world in which both moralists and metaphysicians were just beginning to view truth in relative terms. Like Descartes and Malebranche, like his contemporary Pascal, La Rochefoucauld desperately sought out truth, but in his case the search was carried out without the consolation provided by faith in the Christian God as Truth's ultimate source.[5] Like Pascal, La Rochefoucauld looked around at his world as well as back to his earlier life as a courtier and found much evidence that deceit and falsehood were integral parts of human experience. Like the author of the *Pensées,* he understood that disguise is a fundamental human trait. However, unlike Pascal, La Rochefoucauld saw no obvious solution to the dilemma of the human being, who, as Pascal put it, can neither know everything with total certitude nor be totally ignorant.[6] On the one hand, it is undeniable that the warring convictions with which La Rochefoucauld's work abounds often come close to contradicting each other. On the other hand, it may be true, as Jean Granier contends in his book on the problem of truth in the philosophy of Nietzsche, that "toute grande pensée vit des contradictions qu'elle surmonte—et plus encore, peut-être, des contradictions qu'elle ne surmonte pas" (11) ("every great system of thought lives on the contradictions it surmounts— and even more, perhaps, on the contradictions that it does not surmount").

* * *

In both the *Maximes* and the *Réflexions diverses,* this preoccupation with defining and analyzing the concept of truth manifests itself in different ways, but especially in the frequency with which the noun *vérité* ("truth") and the adjective *vrai,* sometimes substantivized as *le vrai,* occur. In the *Maximes,* the term *vérité* occurs only three times, but the adjective *vrai* and its near synonym *véritable* are much more frequent and are used in a variety of contexts from love to politics.[7] In addition, many more elements of La Rochefoucauld's lexicon are directly or indirectly related to the concept of truth and, often through the idea of deceiving another (or oneself), to the concept of falsehood. One of the main objectives of this study is to identify and analyze those lexical elements and to delimit as precisely as possible the wide variety of contexts in which they are to be found.

In the very first *réflexion* ("Du vrai" ["Of Truth"]), La Rochefoucauld attempts to define truth, both in abstract terms and by using historical and architectural examples. It is highly significant that he chose to place this key text at the very beginning of the *réflexions,* just as Sir Francis Bacon placed "Of Truth" at the beginning of his essays, "civill and morall."[8] The thirteenth *réflexion,* entitled "Du faux" ("Of Falsehood"), presents falsehood as a universal phenomenon, pervading almost every area of human experience. It also provides a brief typology of the various kinds of falsehood and of the many social, psychological, and moral phenomena with which La Rochefoucauld associates the concept.

In La Rochefoucauld's eyes, distinguishing truth from falsehood is an enterprise requiring great effort and powerful insight. They are often very similar in outward appearance and, even more disturbing for the moralist, in social repercussions and moral effect. As Montaigne, one of La Rochefoucauld's favorite authors, wrote in the essay "Des boyteux" ("Of Cripples"),

> La vérité et le mensonge ont leurs visages conformes, le port, le goust et les alleures pareilles; nous les regardons de mesme œil. (1004; see Appendix 1)

La Rochefoucauld goes even further, however, describing truth and falsehood as closely bound up with each other in a complex dialectical relationship that the average person often barely perceives and inevitably fails to understand.[9] Of course, the problem is one that has intrigued philosophers from Plato to Heidegger. However, La Rochefoucauld's approach is particularly fascinating in that he deals with the question not as an abstract philosophical problem but as an integral part of a complex and, on many levels, largely original analysis of human motivation and of the multifaceted life of the Self.

As we shall see in subsequent chapters of this study, La Rochefoucauld views the problem of truth as one aspect of a much larger set of problems arising out of his desire to plumb the depths of the human psyche and to bring to the surface the hidden and perhaps even unconscious forces at work there. Unlike most of his contemporaries, La Rochefoucauld recognizes and tries to assess the wide range of human activity in which the predilection for falsehood and, more importantly, for disguising the true nature of that falsehood, plays a crucial and even decisive role. The world in which the socialized individual must learn to function is, in La Rochefoucauld's estimation, "un jeu de miroirs où le vrai et le faux, l'illusion et la réalité finissent par se confondre" (Dens, "Morale et société" 55) ("a game of mirrors in which truth and falsehood, illusion and reality end up merging one into the other"). The consequences of this profoundly unsettling view of human existence, both for the individual and for society as a whole, constitute a recurrent theme throughout La Rochefoucauld's work.

* * *

The importance La Rochefoucauld attaches to what Francis Jeanson has called the individual's "essentielle fausseté"[10] ("essential falsity") was not lost on even the earliest readers of the *Maximes,* including his close friend and collaborator Mme de Sablé. In a letter to La Rochefoucauld dated 18 February 1665 referring to initial reactions to his book, she discusses the fact that while some readers have objected to the negative image of human nature it projects, "les autres au contraire trouvent ce traité fort utile parce qu'il découvre *les fausses idées que les hommes ont d'eux-mêmes* [emphasis mine] . . ."[11] ("others on the contrary find this treatise very useful because it uncovers *the false ideas which men have about themselves*"). For La Rochefoucauld, of course, the problem is not just that human beings have erroneous or inflated ideas about their own merit, but that they try to convince others that the "false ideas" they have about themselves are true.[12] In his eyes, what makes these kinds of falsehoods so difficult to identify, and therefore so dangerous, is that they are almost always disguised in one way or another, either by being presented as truths—in other words, masked—or by being mixed with truths, in some unknown and perhaps unknowable proportions.

Along similar lines, Paul Bénichou has argued that individuals' propensity for harboring "false ideas" about themselves and at the same time seeking to perpetuate those falsehoods is at the heart of La Rochefoucauld's entire psychology:

> Qu'est-ce à dire, sinon que le spectacle de l'homme lui donne, par une intuition immédiate, le sentiment de la *fausseté,* et que toute sa psychologie n'est que la mise en forme de cette intuition? ("L'Intention des *Maximes*" 22; emphasis mine; see Appendix 2)

As we shall see, La Rochefoucauld's view that falsehoods are dangerous because they are rarely presented or perceived as such is directly related to his theories regarding both the internal and the external forces determining human behavior. Since the search for truth is constantly frustrated by a predisposition for falsehood, human interaction inevitably becomes a long process of role-playing and illusion-making.

* * *

It must be emphasized that the kinds of truths and falsehoods that interest La Rochefoucauld are not usually of a transcendental or metaphysical nature. They have little to do, directly at least, with the eternal truths of Descartes's God. Rather, they tend to be practical, concrete, everyday truths that result from human action and interaction on a day-to-day basis. Jacques Truchet sees La Rochefoucauld's concept of truth as part of his eminently classical desire to see harmony rise out of chaos:

> On remarquera que la vérité dont il s'agit n'est pas trans-
> cendante, d'essence métaphysique, mais relative et pratique:
> chacun doit se maintenir sa vérité, telle qu'elle se trouve
> déterminée par son tempérament, par sa condition, par les
> circonstances. C'est pourquoi elle ne se sépare pas du naturel;
> elle est harmonie, tandis que la fausseté est disproportion.[13]
> (See Appendix 3)

As Louis Van Delft has noted, most French moralists of the
period, including La Rochefoucauld, were not really philosophers in the traditional sense of the word. Their interests were
much more immediate, much more directly concerned with the
here and now and the everyday problems faced by human
beings:

> Même quand ils se désignent du nom de "philosophes," les
> moralistes du XVIIᵉ siècle . . . ne se livrent pas à la spécu-
> lation, à la méta-physique. *Ils se consacrent bien, eux aussi,
> à "la recherche de la vérité,"* mais ce ne sont pas l'éten-
> due, le mouvement, les caractères de la raison, les causes
> occasionnelles qui les retiennent. Le moraliste se tient au
> relatif, au contingent, au concret, à l'accidentel, et par-dessus
> tout au *vécu*. ("La Spécificité" 552; emphasis mine; see
> Appendix 4)

In modern terms, La Rochefoucauld and his fellow seventeenth-
century moralists are much less speculative philosophers than
practicing psychologists. "Their objective is not the great truths
of life, but the painful, the all too human truths of living."[14]
Like Sir Francis Bacon in his famous essay "Of Truth," La
Rochefoucauld was concerned not with "Theologicall, and Philo-
sophicall Truth" but rather with "the Truth of civill Busi-
nesse"(Bacon 8).

The various meanings of the term *vérité* in common usage
in seventeenth-century France, as they are given by the lexicographer Antoine Furetière in his *Dictionnaire universel*
(1690), reflect this fundamental distinction. Furetière's first definition refers to eternal, metaphysical truths:

> VERITÉ. Ce qui est essentiellement vrai. C'est dans cette
> acception qu'on dit, Dieu est la verité même, la verité essen-
> tielle, l'éternelle verité. (See Appendix 5)

Furetière lists another somewhat similar but more general meaning of the term, referring to that which is demonstrably true (scientific truth) or that which is accepted on faith as being true (religious truth):

> VERITÉ, dans un sens plus ordinaire est opposé à erreur, fausse opinion, et signifie, une proposition vraye, et certaine; un dogme constant, et incontestable; une maxime claire, et évidente; connoissance de la nature des choses. On le dit tant par rapport aux mysteres de la Religion, que par rapport aux connoissances que l'on acquiert par l'étude, ou par la meditation. Il faut imprimer de bonne heure dans l'esprit les veritez de la Religion . . . MALEB. Nous cherchons la verité à tâtons: nous n'en voyons que les apparences . . . LA ROCH. *La plus générale division qu'on ait accoutumé de faire de toutes les sectes des Philosophes, est de les distinguer en ceux qui croyoient d'avoir trouvé la verité, ceux qui croyoient qu'elle ne pouvait pas se trouver, et ceux qui croyant ne l'avoir pas trouvée, la cherchoient pourtant toute leur vie* . . . (Emphasis mine; see Appendix 6)

Of the three kinds of "philosopher" referred to in the second example (attributed, interestingly enough, to La Rochefoucauld), I will try to show that La Rochefoucauld saw himself as belonging to the third category, those who may not yet have found the truth (at least not very often) but who have nevertheless untiringly carried out the search.

Furetière's third definition of *vérité* not only provides a precise idea of the kinds of practical everyday truths with which La Rochefoucauld was primarily, although not exclusively, concerned, but also furnishes considerable insight into what La Rochefoucauld's contemporaries saw as the basic contexts or circumstances in which these truths are to be found:

> VERITÉ, se dit encore de la sincerité, de la bonne foi dans le rapport de quelques faits particuliers, ou personnels; des évenemens; des incidens; des circonstances de ce qui se passe: *en ce cas elle est opposée au mensonge, au deguisement, à la fourberie.* L'accusé sçut si bien cacher, et deguiser la verité, qu'on ne put le convaincre d'un crime que personne ne doutoit qu'il n'eût commis . . . NIC. *On voudroit avoir la gloire d'aimer la verité, et la satisfaction de ne l'entendre jamais* . . . (Emphasis mine; see Appendix 7)

This last definition incorporates two of the key elements in La Rochefoucauld's analyses of truth and falsehood, particularly those contained in the *Réflexions diverses:* the idea of truth in a *specific* situation or context and the importance of acting in good faith and in a sincere manner when truths of a personal nature are being passed on or revealed to others.

* * *

Like Montaigne, La Rochefoucauld the moralist is passionately involved in a "conversational search for truth" (Thweatt 243), an enterprise in which, like Montaigne, he no doubt tended to draw on his own personal experiences as well as on his vast literary and philosophical culture. However, his choice of the maxim as a literary form (in a sense, the *Réflexions diverses* are really long maxims, similar to the famous *maxime supprimée* 1 on *l'amour-propre*[15]) resulted in a presentation very different from that of the *Essais.* Unlike Montaigne, who attempted to arrive at basic human truths and universal, timeless values through a detailed examination of his own constantly changing thoughts and beliefs, La Rochefoucauld was much less inclined to reveal to his readers the painful personal truths that systematic introspection sometimes produces. Instead, he provides a distillation of the observations and analyses made by a consummate artist who saw in the maxim the ideal literary form in which to express not his own private truths, as Montaigne had done, but rather the truth as he saw it. La Rochefoucauld was very conscious of the traditional association between the maxim or aphorism as a literary form and the concept of truth. Authors from Marcus Aurelius to Baltasar Gracián (whose *Oráculo manual* has many close affinities with La Rochefoucauld's *Maximes,* and whose work is also dominated by the denunciation of errors and affectations of all kinds and by the search for truth) have understood and exploited the aphorism as a vehicle for expressing basic human truths.

The first readers of the *Maximes,* Mme de Sablé and her circle of acquaintances and correspondents, were quick to make this association as well and saw La Rochefoucauld as first and foremost a purveyor of fundamental human verities. In a letter addressed to Mme de Sablé, Mme de Schonberg expressed her gratitude to La Rochefoucauld for having shown her many hidden truths about human nature:

> il y a en cet ouvrage beaucoup d'esprit, peu de bonté, et *forces vérités* que j'aurais ignorées toute ma vie si l'on ne m'en avait fait apercevoir. (Truchet ed. 564; emphasis mine; see Appendix 8)

In another letter by an unknown reader of the *Maximes,* addressed to Mme de Schonberg and passed on by her to Mme de Sablé, the pleasure of reading La Rochefoucauld is closely linked to the many truths contained in his work:

> c'est un fonds très fertile d'*une infinité de belles vérités* qu'on a le plaisir de découvrir en fouissant un peu par la méditation. (Truchet ed. 569; emphasis mine; see Appendix 9)

These early readers of the *Maximes* perceived that La Rochefoucauld's genius lies not only in his ability to reveal a significant number of truths, but also in his discovery of a powerful means of expressing them for the future instruction and enjoyment of his readers.

Today, the *Maximes* continue to find readers who, like La Rochefoucauld's contemporaries, discover a surprising and even disconcerting number of indisputable, if not always entirely comfortable or unambiguous, truths about the human condition. Indeed, the biologist Jean Rostand has suggested that it may be because La Rochefoucauld puts forth so many unpleasant and unavoidable truths about human nature that he has so often been attacked, beginning in the eighteenth century, as either excessively pessimistic or too overtly cynical about the forces governing human actions and reactions:

> Si les *Maximes,* d'ailleurs, ne contenaient pas, sinon toute la vérité, du moins tant de vérités, pourquoi se fût-on à ce point récrié contre elles? (37; see Appendix 10)

In addition to their literary and artistic merits, the *Maximes* and the *Réflexions diverses* pose, in concise and strikingly modern terms, the fundamental questions about human nature that have preoccupied moralists since ancient times. Though La Rochefoucauld's efforts to unmask the truth may have been methodologically less rigorous than those of his contemporary Descartes, he nevertheless has provided modern readers with many profound insights into the anatomy of the human heart.

Chapter Two

La Rochefoucauld and
the Baroque Worldview

Ainsi la vie humaine n'est qu'une illusion
perpétuelle . . .

Pascal, *Pensée* 743[†]

Il y a une révolution générale qui change le goût
des esprits, aussi bien que les fortunes du monde.
La Rochefoucauld, *Maxime supprimée* 48[‡]

Before we examine in greater detail, through a close reading of his works, La Rochefoucauld's ideas concerning truth and its various masks and disguises, it is of vital importance to place his moral writings in what is by no means the only context in which they can or should be studied, but one with the advantage of providing an important series of keys to understanding his concept of truth—that of the Baroque worldview. Like many of his contemporaries, La Rochefoucauld was profoundly influenced by the fundamental principles, concepts, and modes of representation that characterized Baroque art and literature in western Europe from the mid sixteenth century to the mid seventeenth century. As we shall note in this and subsequent chapters of our study, the Baroque dimensions of La Rochefoucauld's work are numerous, multifaceted and far-reaching, particularly with respect to some of the basic moral and social issues raised by his inquiry into the nature of truth, without necessarily always resolving them (a process that is in itself quintessentially Baroque). From the unseen effects of self-love

---

[†] Thus human life is nothing but a perpetual illusion . . .

[‡] The revolving years change men's intellectual tastes no less than their worldly fortunes.

to the dialectical relationship between vice and virtue, many of La Rochefoucauld's most interesting and most original ideas can best be understood in this context. In other words, the importance of viewing La Rochefoucauld as a Baroque thinker and to some extent as a Baroque writer lies in the fact that by so doing, it is possible to see not only where the most important elements of his concept of truth originated but also how they are related to each other.

Before taking a closer look at the Baroque underpinnings of La Rochefoucauld's work, let us briefly retrace the steps by which the term *Baroque,* which originated in art history, came to be applied, as a set of critical concepts and categories, to literary works as diverse in content and outlook as Montaigne's *Essais* and Rotrou's plays, as different in origin, tone, and form as the writings of Gracián and the comedies of Corneille. It is by no means a coincidence that the first modern critic to apply the term *Baroque* to La Rochefoucauld (and at the same time to call into question the moralist's long-accepted status as a "classical writer") was Jean Rousset, whose book *La Littérature de l'âge baroque en France* began what is to this day a vigorous debate on the validity (and even to some extent the meaning) of the term *Baroque* as it has been applied to literary texts. In applying the "catégories critiques" that Rousset, Claude-Gilbert Dubois, and others[1] first established for use in studying Baroque texts, I have chosen to adopt the stance that Rousset himself advocates: to use the concept of Baroque as a critical tool "d'exploration et de sondage" ("of exploration and probing"), keeping in mind at all times "son caractère d'hypothèse de travail: un outil pour questionner la réalité" (*L'Intérieur et l'extérieur* 248) ("its status as a working hypothesis: a tool for investigating reality"). As Rousset convincingly argues, such concepts must always be tested, and their validity ultimately determined, by the extent to which they help us understand the texts to which we apply them.

Recently, the debate begun in the 1950s by Rousset over the nature and the validity of the concept of the Baroque has once again become a lively one. Guy Scarpetta's book *L'Artifice* (1988), for example, presents the Baroque as a set of aesthetic principles and practices that originated in the seventeenth and eighteenth centuries but that have reappeared in modern culture, in the work of Picasso and Carlos Fuentes, among others. It is Scarpetta's contention that this "retour . . . d'une veine baroque" (12) ("return of a Baroque vein") in contemporary culture has touched, as it did in La Rochefoucauld's and in Vivaldi's time, virtually every area of artistic and intellectual life, from painting and music to literature and philosophy. In a similar manner, Gilles Deleuze's *Le Pli: Leibniz et le baroque*[2] (1988) assumes that the Baroque is rooted in a coherent worldview that formed the basis for much of European culture in the so-called Age of Reason, and that is very much alive today. In the introduction to "Baroque Topographies: Literature/History/ Philosophy," his recent special issue of *Yale French Studies,* Timothy Hampton summarizes the modern view of the Baroque as involving (1) "a particular set of stylistic traits," (2) "an aesthetics of conflict," and (3) "a particular mode of representation employing paradox, illusionism, . . . and so on" (3). It is in the light of this revitalized debate about, and redefinition of, the nature of the Baroque that I intend to consider the impact of Baroque culture on La Rochefoucauld.

Although La Rochefoucauld's work is most often associated with the aesthetic values of French classicism, it is also unquestionably imbued with the spirit and the tone as well as, in many instances, the sensibility and the substance of European High Baroque. Like Racine, La Rochefoucauld was essentially a classical writer, but, like the dramatist, he was nevertheless profoundly influenced by Baroque literature, particularly by his reading of *L'Astrée* (1607–19), Honoré d'Urfé's five-thousand-page novel, and of Montaigne's *Essais,* and by his more-than-passing familiarity with Italian Baroque theater. It should be emphasized here, however, that the Baroque underpinnings to La Rochefoucauld's work go far beyond questions of the influence of d'Urfé or Montaigne (or Gracián and Guarini for that matter) on the *Maximes.* La Rochefoucauld's debt to the Baroque encompasses a number of aesthetic concerns and stylistic features as well as a wide range of moral, social, and even metaphysical concepts and issues. What makes the Baroque aspects of La Rochefoucauld's work so interesting, especially to the modern reader, is that when the author of the *Maximes* takes as a starting point a fundamentally Baroque concept, such as life as theater, he never fails to adapt the idea to his own aesthetic and ideological purposes, to use it in a way at once strongly reminiscent of the Baroque and uniquely his own.

At the level of form as well as content, many aspects of La Rochefoucauld's work are unquestionably Baroque, both in origin and in essence.[3] His style is heavily infused with Baroque rhetorical devices (antithesis and hyperbole, among others) and a number of other related stylistic features.[4] As is often the case with some of the other *figures de rhétorique* he employs, La Rochefoucauld's use of antithesis is not just a rhetorical strategy. Rather, it is deeply rooted in his tendency to see reality in terms of stark contrast between opposites: light and dark, truth and falsehood, vice and virtue. This proclivity for seeing not just physical reality but also moral values and even modes of social behavior in terms of what Didier Souiller has called "des antithèses non résolues" (*La Littérature baroque en Europe* 65–126) ("unresolved antitheses") is undoubtedly Baroque in origin. What La Rochefoucauld most often does in such cases is to take a fundamental Baroque concept and apply it to areas of human experience to which it has not previously been applied. At the level of imagery, one also finds in the *Maximes* a large number of images in which the tenor and vehicle are shockingly disparate in nature, in which the metaphor is based on an unfamiliar or unexpected way of looking at reality or on the establishment of connections between normally unrelated concepts and areas of human experience. Images of this kind are, of course, to be found throughout Baroque literature, in the poems of Théophile de Viau and John Donne and in the prose of Montaigne and Sir Thomas Browne.[5]

On another level, the "discontinuous" nature of La Rochefoucauld's prose can also be seen in the context of Baroque aesthetic values and principles, these in turn being related to more general presuppositions about the nature of reality. Like Montaigne's *Essais,* the *Maximes* display the same discursive "internal discontinuity" (Lafond, "Des formes brèves" 117) that characterizes much of Baroque literature, regardless of genre. While many literary historians tend to see the *maxime* as an eminently classical form (one that realizes the classical ideal of "saying everything in few words" ["tout dire en peu de mots"]), the *Maximes* as a whole (whether read in isolation from each other or as a single text) do indeed exhibit the internal discontinuity that is a basic characteristic of the Baroque not to mention modern(ist) literature. Underlying La Rochefoucauld's use of the *maxime* as a literary form is a fundamental paradox: in order to transpose into words a reality that is both transitory and illusory, to capture in concise and concrete form a reality that is both diffuse and elusive, La Rochefoucauld makes use of a form that, like the sonnet, is fixed, rigid, and by its very nature static. This paradox is at the very heart of Baroque aesthetic theory.

According to Gisèle Mathieu-Castellani, one of the primary objectives of Baroque discourse, with its characteristic discontinuity and fluidity, is to convince or persuade the reader by shocking him or her into radically new modes of perception and cognition. It is for this reason that the rhetorical strategies that Baroque discourse systematically employs, including discontinuity, inevitably lead the unsuspecting reader to reflect on the nature of truth:

> Le discours baroque—et c'est là son caractère dominant—s'attache à convaincre ou à persuader . . . , à provoquer une adhésion intellectuelle et/ou affective. *Mais ce discours persuasif se donne aussi comme un discours de la Vérité.* (Mathieu-Castellani 21; emphasis mine; see Appendix 11)

In other words, the stylistic and other formal elements of the Baroque text work together to force readers to re-examine their own concept of truth. It is because of this vital link between the very nature of Baroque discourse and the problem of truth that the Baroque context of La Rochefoucauld's work cannot be ignored.

Even critics like Corrado Rosso, who have expressed considerable reservations about the validity of referring to La Rochefoucauld as a Baroque writer,[6] concede that although the author of the *Maximes* may be most accurately described as an "eminently classical writer," he nevertheless "maintains close links with Baroque civilization."[7] This Baroque dimension to La Rochefoucauld's work appears most clearly at the thematic level, where a number of typically Baroque concerns, from appearances and reality and *inconstance* to metamorphosis and death, reappear in a new and strikingly original form. Without question, it is more than the delight in paradox that attracted La Rochefoucauld to Baroque literature and led him to use Baroque themes and imagery as a starting point for many of his most noteworthy *maximes* and *réflexions*.[8] What makes La Rochefoucauld's work remarkable in this respect is that one often discovers in it, as sometimes in Racine, "the shifting complexity of the Baroque beneath the controlled proportion of Classical form" (Thweatt 215). Even when the style of a passage of La Rochefoucauld displays the balance and equilibrium associated with the literature of French classicism, the subject matter is often, as W. G. Moore has suggested, "new, baffling, astounding, paradoxical, a scandal to the intelligence" ("La Rochefoucauld's Masterpiece" 268)—in a word, Baroque.

* * *

To understand fully the intellectual climate in which La Rochefoucauld was working when he approached the problem of truth and falsehood in the *Maximes* and in the *Réflexions diverses,* one must not lose sight of the Baroque origins and overtones of two of his favorite themes: illusion (and the related concepts of disguise and deceit) and inconstancy, the fundamental instability and mutability of both Nature and human life. In La Rochefoucauld, as in much of Baroque literature, appearances are always a means of deceiving others (and oneself) and falsehoods are blatantly and routinely passed off as truths, even by one's closest friends. However, in Baroque literature, appearances tend to be associated with external reality as perceived by the individual. Even in dream sequences such as the premonitions experienced by Thisbé's mother in Théophile de Viau's *Pyrame et Thisbé* (1623) or Francion's famous dream in Sorel's *Histoire comique de Francion* (1623), the illusory images that pass through the Subject's consciousness have much more to do with the perception, however distorted it may be, of objective reality than with the internal and unconscious illusion-making that La Rochefoucauld sees as a basic characteristic of human life. Throughout the *Maximes,* La Rochefoucauld takes the Baroque concept of illusion and, for the first time in French intellectual history, single-mindedly applies it to the highly subjective area of human motivation, to the underlying forces and processes that determine people's behavior, often without their knowledge or consent. As we shall see, La Rochefoucauld often describes situations in which illusions are created or some form of deception carried out by people's self-love or their laziness and without any conscious or deliberate effort on their part.

Like Pascal, La Rochefoucauld sees the individual, alone and in society, as both the victim and the culprit in the never-ending process of deception and delusion in which human beings constantly indulge:

> L'homme n'est donc que déguisement, que mensonge et hypocrisie, et en soi-même et à l'égard des autres. Il ne veut pas qu'on lui dise la vérité, il évite de la dire aux autres . . . (*Pensée* 743, Pascal 436; see Appendix 12)

Both La Rochefoucauld and Pascal derived this principle from several sources, including classical literature and theology, but their most important source was Baroque literature.[9] Characteristically, La Rochefoucauld goes much farther than Pascal in his analysis of the individual's innate predilection for dissembling and concealing real feelings and motivations, for feigning and showing false colors. It is La Rochefoucauld's contention that the continual production of illusions takes place in virtually every sphere of human activity. As a result, life becomes a struggle to understand and to cope with a world in which nothing is ever what it seems. Henri Coulet sees this aspect of La Rochefoucauld's thought as both one of the great paradoxes of the *Maximes* and an important key to understanding the moral philosophy behind them:

> Dans cette atmosphère, les *Maximes* de La Rochefoucauld représentent un effort hautain, mais secrètement impuissant, pour sauver la grandeur de l'homme en restant dans une défiance minutieuse et systématique à l'égard de toute illusion. (105; see Appendix 13)

One of the moralist's main tasks thus becomes the denunciation of all illusions, both individual and collective. At the same time, for the well-being of each individual member of society, the moralist must strive to reveal the profound consequences of a social system based, as La Rochefoucauld saw it, on wide-spread fraudulence and deceit, on a process of illusion-making that is much more than an idle pastime. This task is facilitated, as Francis Jeanson points out, by the moralist's exceptional ability to discern illusion and uncover reality beneath the veil of appearances:

> s'il demeure entendu que les hommes n'ont au lieu d'esprit qu'une permanente illusion, le moraliste, lui, se trouve doué d'une sorte de transcendance par rapport à ce chaos d'illusions individuelles. (77; see Appendix 14)

In theory, at least, the clairvoyance and lucidity that characterize the moralist should enable him or her to deal much more effectively than other people do with the surrounding illusory world, simply because of a better understanding of the process of illusion-making than others can ever hope to attain.

* * *

Like the theme of illusion, another of La Rochefoucauld's favorite themes, inconstancy, has deep roots in the Baroque world-view. In the seventeenth century, the term *inconstance* was used in two principal contexts: first, individuals' subjective view of themselves and their surroundings (including tastes, likes and dislikes, opinions, passions) and, second, external reality (including society, nature, and that most fickle of external forces, fortune). Both contexts emerge very clearly in the definitions of *inconstance* and *inconstant(e)* that Furetière provides in his *Dictionnaire universel* (1690):

> INCONSTANCE. s. f. Manque de fermeté, de durée, de resolution. L'*inconstance* est un vice de l'âme qui la fait changer quelquefois en pis, quelquefois en mieux. (See Appendix 15)

> INCONSTANT, ante. adj. Qui n'a point de fermeté, de constance. La fortune est *inconstante*. [L]es amans sont d'ordinaire *inconstants*. (See Appendix 16)

For Furetière and his contemporaries, *inconstance* is thus primarily a lack of psychological stability, a profoundly human tendency to change both one's mind and the object of one's affections, "a defect of the soul." In a much wider context, the term also refers to a fundamental characteristic both of society, which necessarily reflects the instability of its members, and of nature as a whole, as many Baroque poets (Etienne Durand, in his "Stances à l'inconstance," for example) had shown. La Rochefoucauld understood, perhaps better than many of his contemporaries, that in both private and public life, inconstancy is a fundamental element of human existence, a fact that the Fronde had so clearly and, for La Rochefoucauld, so tragically, illustrated.

It is therefore not surprising that the concept of *inconstance* appears in La Rochefoucauld's works in many forms and guises. The word itself appears in several *maximes* (and an entire *réflexion diverse* [XVII] is devoted to the topic), but the concept can be found elsewhere any time La Rochefoucauld describes or discusses the ever-present human predilection for movement and change, for what he sometimes calls "révolutions."[10] The idea that we are continually subject to movement and change, both internally and externally, is related to La Rochefoucauld's belief that human beings are at the mercy of physical and psychological forces that they are unable to control (or even to understand), that "les hommes sont livrés aux forces les plus élémentaires de la nature qui les meuvent à leur insu et les ballottent sans cesse" (Baker, *Collaboration et originalité* 85) ("men are at the mercy of the most elementary forces of nature, which move them around at their will and batter them incessantly"). Life is always forcing them to adapt to new situations. Even mature adults often lack the experience and the flexibility necessary to cope with constant change:

> Nous arrivons tout nouveaux aux divers âges de la vie, et nous y manquons souvent d'expérience malgré le nombre des années. (M 405; see Appendix 17)

At every stage in their development, human beings are faced with new obstacles to be overcome and find themselves forced to adapt to rapidly evolving circumstances. It is little wonder that they are always changing their minds. Indeed, such changeability is perfectly understandable:

> Il y a une *inconstance* qui vient de la légèreté de l'esprit ou de sa faiblesse, qui lui fait recevoir toutes les opinions d'autrui, et il y en a une autre, qui est plus excusable, qui vient du dégoût des choses. (M 181; emphasis mine; see Appendix 18)

What makes La Rochefoucauld's view of this aspect of human nature substantially different from that of most of his contemporaries—and at the same time remarkably modern—is his emphasis on the fact that human beings are often completely unaware of the degree to which instability characterizes almost every area of experience. As Jean Rousset points out in an early article, La Rochefoucauld believes that human inconstancy is routinely invisible to those who suffer from it: "il y a bien un centre en nous, mais un centre caché, fuyant, inconnu à nous-mêmes . . ." ("La Rochefoucauld contre le classicisme" 108) ("there is definitely a center in each of us, but it is a center that is hidden, elusive, unknown to ourselves . . .").

Not only love and jealousy but also tastes in many other aspects of daily life are subject to what Barthes has called "les contingences," the myriad of changing circumstances and chance happenings that all human beings constantly face.[11] Personal tastes, both emotional and intellectual, evolve, just as events evolve in the surrounding world:

> Il y a une *révolution* générale qui change le goût des esprits, aussi bien que les fortunes du monde. (MS 48; emphasis mine; see Appendix 19)

That eternal source of illusion, self-love, along with our changing moods forces us to see and feel what is going on around us in new, and sometimes disturbingly different, ways:

> Personne ne voit des mêmes yeux ce qui le touche et ce qui ne le touche pas; notre goût est conduit alors par la pente de l'amour-propre et de l'humeur, qui nous fournissent des vues nouvelles, et nous assujettissent à *un nombre infini de changements et d'incertitudes;* notre goût n'est plus à nous, nous n'en disposons plus, il change notre consentement, et les mêmes objets nous paraissent par tant de côtés différents que nous méconnaissons enfin ce que nous avons vu et ce

que nous avons senti. ("Des goûts," RD 203; emphasis mine;
see Appendix 20)

This "infinite number of changes and uncertainties," which
permanently weaken our resolve and ultimately "enslave" us,
is part of a much larger (and eminently Baroque) view of life.
In the case of our tastes and "humors," what is most disconcerting about this process is that "our taste is no longer ours."
We are no longer in control of our likes and dislikes, for they
are subject to modifications as imperceptible as they are
inexorable.

Like many of his contemporaries, La Rochefoucauld at
times attributes this psychological instability to physical causes,
most notably the ever-changing humors, the four liquids that,
according to Aristotelian medicine, "abreuvent tous les corps
des animaux, & qu'on croit estre causes des divers tempe-
ramments" (Furetière, "Humeur") ("are found in the bodies of
animals, and which are believed to be the causes of the various temperaments"). In his *The Anatomy of Melancholy* (1621),
Robert Burton defines a humor as:

> a liquid or fluent part of the Body, comprehended in it, for
> the preservation of it, . . . either innate or borne with us, or
> adventitious and acquisite . . . These foure humours have
> some analogie with the foure Elements, and to the foure ages
> in man. (1: 140–41)

According to what was, at the time, a widely accepted theory,
these four substances, which are in constant motion, can, in
addition to producing or altering an individual's temperament,
cause profound, but usually imperceptible, changes in our mental
and emotional states:

> Les humeurs du corps ont un cours ordinaire et réglé, *qui*
> *meut et qui tourne imperceptiblement notre volonté; elles*
> *roulent ensemble* et exercent successivement un empire secret
> en nous: de sorte qu'elles ont une part considérable à toutes
> nos actions, sans que nous le puissions connaître. (M 297;
> emphasis mine; see Appendix 21)

What is most significant about the "secret" power of the humors is, in La Rochefoucauld's eyes, the fact that human beings

perceive only their external manifestations, not their true nature:

> Nous ne nous apercevons que *des emportements et des mouvements extraordinaires de nos humeurs,* comme de la violence, de la colère, etc. . . . (Liancourt 50; emphasis mine; see Appendix 22)

Furthermore, La Rochefoucauld sees in "the passions that move around in us according to the disposition or movement of these four humors" ("[l]es passions qui s'esmeuvent en nous suivant la disposition ou l'agitation de ces quatre *humeurs*") (Furetière, "Humeur") one of the primary reasons why love, like all human emotions, is so subject to change.[12]

In addition to our changing feelings and emotions, there is, of course, that other great *contingence,* fortune, which works, sometimes in concert with the humors but more often in conflict with them, and further increases the uncertainty with which all human beings must face the future. Like the faculty of the imagination, which, as Pascal perceived, is an even greater source of illusion and error because it is not always one, fortune, as La Rochefoucauld clearly demonstrates, is in a sense even more capricious because it occasionally "renounces" its capriciousness to work in concert with Nature:

> Il semble que la fortune, *toute changeante et capricieuse qu'elle est,* renonce à ces changements et à ces caprices pour agir de concert avec la nature, et que l'une et l'autre concourent de temps en temps à faire des hommes extraordinaires et singuliers, pour servir de modèles à la postérité. ("Des modèles de la nature et de la fortune," RD 210; emphasis mine; see Appendix 23)

Unfortunately, even exceptional human beings cannot escape the unseen (and unforeseen) forces of chance, what Barthes has called the "hasard des événements" (*Nouveaux essais critiques* 81) ("the fortuitous nature of events"):

> La mort même de M. de Turenne, si convenable à une si belle vie, accompagnée de tant de circonstances singulières et arrivée dans un moment si important, ne nous paraît-elle pas comme un effet de la crainte et de *l'incertitude de la*

fortune, qui n'a osé décider de la destinée de la France et
de l'Empire? ("Des modèles de la nature et de la fortune,"
RD 214; emphasis mine; see Appendix 24)

It is true that in the second half of the seventeenth century,
commenting upon the uncertainty of fortune and its effects is
hardly, in itself, very original, as Mascarille's ironic (and comic)
outburst, "O Fortune, such is your inconstancy!" ("O Fortune,
quelle est ton inconstance!"), at the end of Molière's *Les Pré-
cieuses ridicules* (1659) aptly illustrates. However, La Rochefoucauld's frequent and often ambiguous pronouncements on
the subject, when viewed in the context of his concept of *inconstance,* do provide some interesting, but profoundly pessimistic, variations on an old theme.

* * *

In this ever-changing world of illusion, in which reality is almost always cloaked in an intricate network of illusions and
time inexorably transforms both external reality and our perception of it, La Rochefoucauld sees the Self, not as a unified
and coherent entity, but as a face that wears a thousand masks
and often switches from one to the other in a vain attempt to
keep up with the constant changes going on in the world around
it. In La Rochefoucauld's eyes, the Self is an actor who has
played, and will continue to play, an almost infinite number of
roles. It is not that the life of the Self is unstructured but rather
that the structures involved are extremely complex and in a state
of perpetual movement. In other words, La Rochefoucauld
conceives the heterogeneous nature and the underlying and deep-
seated dynamism and instability of the Self in what are essentially Baroque terms. Nowhere in the *Maximes* are the Baroque
overtones of his portrait of the Self more evident than in the
maxime supprimée 1, which describes, in a typically Baroque
profusion of detail, the secret machinations of that indefatigable
other Self, self-love. Vivien Thweatt has described this text as
Baroque, both in form and in content:

> This is a Baroque structure, and the movement and meta-
> morphoses, the kaleidoscopic succession of deceptive masks,
> the instability and enumerative heaping, the personification,

the prestidigitation, and the fugitive fluidity of its multifaceted poetic expression mark the study itself as a Baroque
composition. (115)

Unlike most of his contemporaries, La Rochefoucauld contends
that the Self is made up of a multiplicity of selves, each one of
which is created and motivated by self-love, by one of an almost infinite number of passions, by motivations and impulses
of which the individual may be only dimly aware.

To the modern reader, familiar with the theories of Freud
and Lacan, such a view of the "radical heterogeneity of the self"
(Laude 532) is perfectly understandable. In La Rochefoucauld's
time, it was a shockingly new, potentially subversive, and, for
a variety of reasons, extremely dangerous idea. If the Self has
not one, but multiple identities, and if these various "selves"
are constantly evolving and often at odds with each other, what
do human will and constancy become in the face of adversity?
And what about the individual's relationship to God? Although
La Rochefoucauld's concept of the Self and its relationship to
others and to the world raises many questions, some of the most
disturbing consequences of La Rochefoucauld's deeply rooted
affinities with the Baroque worldview involve, as we shall see,
his never-ending search for truth. Like Pascal, La Rochefoucauld
depicts the individual as a potentially rational creature in desperate need of certainty and stability in a fundamentally uncertain and unstable world. At the same time, he believes, like
Descartes, that distinguishing between truth and falsehood is
one of the most pressing problems that the individual must face.
Since both truth and falsehood are often heavily disguised and
reality is in a state of constant flux, the task of distinguishing
truth from falsehood with any degree of consistency and in any
truly meaningful way constitutes one of the greatest challenges
facing humanity.

Chapter Three

Truth and Its Masks

In Search of *l'Etre Vrai*

> *Madame de La Fayette me disait que de toutes les*
> *louanges qu'on lui avait données, rien ne lui avait*
> *plu davantage que deux choses que je lui avais*
> *dites: qu'elle avait le jugement au-dessus de son*
> *esprit, et qu'elle aimait le vrai en toutes choses, et*
> *sans dissimulation. C'est ce qui a fait dire à*
> *Monsieur de La Rochefoucauld qu'elle était vraie,*
> *façon de parler dont il est auteur, et qui est assez*
> *en usage.*
>
> Segrais, *Segraisiana*[†]

In La Rochefoucauld's eyes, our eternal search for truth, in a wide range of areas but particularly in the illusory world of human motivations and human interaction, is continually being thwarted by the many masks that, for a multitude of reasons, we social creatures constantly find it advantageous, and even necessary, to make and wear. La Rochefoucauld believes that like true friendship and true love, there does exist the *être vrai* ("genuine person") who is concealed beneath the many disguises human beings routinely deploy, both consciously and unconsciously. This *être vrai* appears in so many different guises, however, that unmasking it is extremely difficult. The *Maximes* repeatedly demonstrate that even those we are closest to, our

---

[†] Madame de La Fayette told me that of all the praise she had received, nothing had pleased her more than two things I said to her: that her judgment was above her wit and that she loved truth in all things, and without dissimulation. This is what made Monsieur de La Rochefoucauld say that she was a genuine person, an expression which he coined, and which is in common usage.

lovers or our best friends, very often succeed in hiding from us their true feelings. The image we have of their character and tastes is therefore inevitably false on one level or another, since it is based on the cleverly disguised falsehoods we all use to mask our real motives and our true identity, both from ourselves and from others.

La Rochefoucauld is not, of course, the first moralist to use mask as metaphor. Indeed, throughout Baroque literature, masks are a powerful symbol not just of the theatricality of life but also, on a much deeper level, of the illusory nature of the face most people present, metaphorically speaking, to the world.[1] In Montaigne, for example, the idea of masking one's true identity—or having it masked by some illusion-making internal or external force—and the necessity of tearing off the mask to reveal the seldom-seen face concealed beneath it appear frequently. In the essay "De la coutume" ("On Habit"), Montaigne uses the concept of the mask to describe the various ways in which experience (*l'usage*) falsifies our perception of reality and effectively prevents us from gaining access to the truth:

> ce masque arraché, rapportant les choses à la vérité et à la raison, il [l'homme] sentira son jugement comme tout bouleversé, et remis pourtant en bien plus seur estat.[2]
> (Montaigne, *Œuvres complètes* 1.23; see Appendix 25)

Like Pascal, Montaigne sees habit as a source of delusion, both of ourselves and of others. Without our knowledge, habit forces us to wear a mask that inhibits our ability to perceive reality and to make sound moral judgments based on that perception. According to La Rochefoucauld, however, many other, more powerful, *puissances trompeuses* are at work, surreptitiously performing the same function. Metaphorically speaking, each of them makes us wear a mask that, in addition to hindering our own powers of perception, also presents a false front to the outside world.

Similarly, in the English moralist Daniel Dyke's *The Mystery of Selfe-deceiving; or, A Discourse and Discovery of the Deceitfulness of Mans Heart,* which La Rochefoucauld probably read in the translation by Jean Vernueil, published in Geneva in 1634 under the title *La Sonde de la conscience,*[3] the act of masking and unmasking (oneself or others) is often associated with moral matters rather than with the theater or masked balls. Like La Rochefoucauld, Dyke is keenly interested in the hidden motives and secret vices that masquerade as virtues. According to Dyke, when one's true feelings or real motivation must for whatever reason be revealed, it is better that the revelation be brought about by the individual concerned, rather than by someone else: ". . . if thine owne hand shall unmaske thee, it shall bee for thy credit . . ." (36). In seventeenth-century France, as in England, the term *mask* was commonly used with a number of figurative meanings. Pierre Richelet's definition in his *Dictionnaire françois,* for example, makes it quite clear that the range of meanings of the word *masque* goes far beyond the literal level:

> MASQUE. Morceau de velours noir où l'on fait un nez et deux yeux dont les Dames se couvrent le visage quand elles vont en campagne, ou en ville.
> ———. Ce mot au figuré a d'autres sens fort beaux.
> ———. Son honnêteté n'est qu'un *masque* pour tromper plus finement. (See Appendix 26)

Without actually using the word *mask* itself, La Rochefoucauld systematically applies the concept to many forms of human behavior, in which the primary objective is not to reveal one's true character and objectives, but rather to conceal them, as effectively and as frequently as possible. The problem is not just that we all pass off falsehoods as truths, but that we deftly and quite deliberately disguise the fact that they are falsehoods. Disguised falsehoods of any kind, La Rochefoucauld believes, are infinitely more dangerous than falsehoods that are easily recognizable as such.

La Rochefoucauld argues that the face most human beings present to the world is not merely a veil concealing the real one, but also a mask designed to present the individual as something he or she is not. Reason can be a mask for unreason, virtue a mask for vice, passion a mask for indifference. Consequently, as Jean Starobinski has pointed out, taking up the cause of truth in such circumstances can become a hazardous enterprise:

> Il semble qu'il soit dangereux de vouloir entrer en guerre
> contre les masques. A prendre contre eux le parti de la *vérité,*
> on résiste mal à la tentation de se donner le beau rôle, qui
> est quelquefois trop beau, et dont la beauté apparaît comme
> celle d'un masque aux yeux de l'ennemi vigilant. Il n'est
> pas rare, en effet, que le défenseur de la vérité se laisse gagner
> par une sorte d'excès où la vérité ne trouve plus son compte.
> ("La Rochefoucauld ou l'oubli des secrets" 34; see Appen-
> dix 27)

In denouncing the infinite variety of masks we all wear, the
moralist becomes vulnerable to the charge of self-aggrandizement. In the resulting furor, the cause being proclaimed may
be quickly forgotten—precisely the fate of La Rochefoucauld,
particularly in the eighteenth century, when his efforts to promote the cause of truth were often seen as both cynical and,
ironically, self-serving.

* * *

The reasons for the consistent and unceasing need of individuals
to mask their true intentions, motives, feelings, and thoughts
from themselves and from others are, in La Rochefoucauld's
analysis of human nature, as complex and varied as human
nature itself. In the *réflexion* "Du faux," La Rochefoucauld
explains at considerable length that the individual's underlying essential falsity can manifest itself in many different ways
and on many different levels:

> On est faux en différentes manières. Il y a des hommes faux
> qui veulent toujours paraître ce qu'ils ne sont pas. Il y en a
> d'autres, de meilleure foi, qui sont nés faux, qui se trompent
> eux-mêmes, et qui ne voient jamais les choses comme elles
> sont. Il y en a dont l'esprit est droit, et le goût faux. D'autres
> ont l'esprit faux, et ont quelque droiture dans le goût. Et il
> y en a qui n'ont rien de faux dans le goût, ni dans l'esprit.
> Ceux-ci sont très rares, puisque, à parler généralement,
> il n'y a presque personne qui n'ait de la fausseté dans
> quelque endroit de l'esprit ou du goût. (RD 207–08; see
> Appendix 28)

The problem is not simply that some people are true and others false but rather that the extent to which all people are false

varies widely from one individual to another as do the ways in which their falsity can affect their mind or compromise their judgment. What makes the task of assessing the degree to which friends and enemies are true or false so problematic is the almost infinite number of ways in which, and degrees to which, they reveal themselves as one or the other.

In the same passage of "Du faux," La Rochefoucauld briefly explores what he believes to be some of the underlying causes of this intrinsic falsity of human beings. As we shall see, many of the *Maximes* as well as some of the other *réflexions* develop and elaborate the author's theory of falsity as a basic human characteristic. In "Du faux," he provides only a brief outline of the reasons why falsehood is such a universal phenomenon:

> Ce qui fait cette fausseté si universelle, c'est que nos qualités sont incertaines et confuses, et que nos vues le sont aussi; on ne voit point les choses précisément comme elles sont, on les estime plus ou moins qu'elles ne valent, et on ne les fait point rapporter à nous en la manière qui leur convient, et qui convient à notre état et à nos qualités. Ce mécompte met un nombre infini de faussetés dans le goût et dans l'esprit: notre amour-propre est flatté de tout ce qui se présente à nous sous les apparences du bien; mais comme il y a plusieurs sortes de biens qui touchent notre vanité ou notre tempérament, on les suit souvent par coutume, ou par commodité; on les suit parce que les autres les suivent, sans considérer qu'un même sentiment ne doit pas être également embrassé par toute sorte de personnes, et qu'on s'y doit attacher plus ou moins fortement selon qu'il convient plus ou moins à ceux qui le suivent. (RD 208; see Appendix 29)

Because our perceptions of reality are often inaccurate and undependable, the judgments we make about reality and the ways in which we react to it are equally unreliable and subject to error. As is often the case in La Rochefoucauld, one of the most important considerations for the moralist is the extent to which our subjective reactions to external reality are appropriate both to ourselves as individuals and to the circumstances of the moment. Since the Self is a multifaceted entity, and the circumstances around us are constantly changing, making appropriate choices and avoiding misjudgments and errors can be difficult objectives to achieve. Errors of judgment are even more likely to occur if, behind the scenes, our self-love is at work, promoting our self-interest and at the same time both distorting our perceptions and, whenever it is possible, intervening in order to influence directly and decisively the choices we make and the decisions we take.

Other moralists of the time, like the Jansenist Pierre Nicole, commented at length on the importance of promoting truth rather than falsehood, of making sound judgments rather than allowing oneself to be taken in by the often illusory nature of external reality. However, unlike La Rochefoucauld, Nicole tended to see the problem of truth not in the practical, everyday terms in which the author of the *Maximes* viewed it but rather in the context of a higher reality, of the necessity of an overriding principle, such as belief in God:

> Il faut nécessairement qu'il y ait quelque voix entendue, c'est-à-dire quelque maxime vraie ou fausse dont notre esprit est persuadé, qui soit le principe de notre vie. C'est la nature et l'essence de tous les êtres intelligents, de se conduire par une lumière qu'ils connoissent; et c'est ce que j'appelle voix. *Leur bonheur est d'être conduit par la voix de la vérité. Leur malheur est de se laisser aller à la voix de la fausseté.* Ainsi le devoir des hommes est d'être continuellement attentifs à la voix de la vérité pour la suivre; et leur dérèglement consiste à écouter et à suivre la voix de la fausseté. (3: 114; emphasis mine; see Appendix 30)

For Nicole, the problem of truth is greatly simplified, and ultimately resolved, in terms of the Cartesian metaphor of the light and the biblical metaphor of the voice, both of which God provides to all those who have lost their way in the impenetrable darkness of human ignorance. In La Rochefoucauld, no such voice, no such overriding principle, exists. No light, metaphorical or literal, ever reaches the struggling to guide them and to encourage them to hear and heed the voice of truth.

* * *

Because relationships between human beings are based almost exclusively on perpetrating falsehoods and exchanging lies, La Rochefoucauld emphasizes again and again that discovering the true nature of an individual involves a difficult and com-

plicated process of unmasking, of peeling off the various layers of pretense and illusion in order to reveal the genuine person hidden underneath. The first and most painful step in the
search for this genuine person requires each of us to recognize
in ourselves the different forms of illusion that we harbor within
us and that can seriously impede our attempts to discern and
reveal the illusions produced, and concealed, by others.[4] This
idea that the true nature of every individual is cloaked in as-
sorted layers of disguise has reappeared from time to time in
French literature, notably in André Gide's *L'Immoraliste* (*The
Immoralist,* 1902), in which the protagonist, Michel, suddenly
discovers that underneath the camouflage of learned values and
attitudes worn by modern man lies a much more natural, spon-
taneous, and, above all, freedom-loving individual. While La
Rochefoucauld is definitely not advocating, as Gide was later
to do, a process of total liberation from the values and the con-
ventions of society, he does nevertheless suggest that life in
society actively encourages, and in some instances forces, individuals to project to the world images of themselves and their
motives that are deliberately falsified.

Although this preoccupation with identifying the genuine
person who lies hidden in each of us can be seen as resulting
from a very negative and even profoundly pessimistic view of
human nature, it can also be considered in a much more positive light, as an attempt to achieve a high degree of lucidity
with respect to our own motives as well as those of others. Henri
Coulet sees this passionate desire for lucidity as a highly significant aspect of La Rochefoucauld's thought:

> Mais on se tromperait en croyant que la seule intention de
> La Rochefoucauld fût de dénigrer l'homme; au contraire,
> dans une tension extrême, il aspire à la liberté en éliminant
> par une critique rigoureuse toute illusion: idéal si difficile
> à atteindre que le monde de la vraie grandeur n'est plus
> aperçu presque que par son absence, monde fermé dont les
> habitants, jalousement triés, ont peur de le laisser dégrader
> par ceux qui en sont indignes, et d'abord par une défaillance
> toujours possible de leur lucidité. (111–12; see Appendix 31)

Like Montaigne, La Rochefoucauld sees our only effective
means of attaining the lucidity we humans so desperately need

as resulting from this complex "critique rigoureuse." With a high degree of lucidity comes a large measure of personal freedom. Difficult and arduous as the attempt to eliminate all forms of illusion and deceit may be, La Rochefoucauld believes unequivocally that the process is essential to our well-being and to our understanding of the world around us. In this respect, La Rochefoucauld is typical of his times.

Ultimately, the total elimination of all falsehoods depends on the individual's willingness to suppress the innate desire to make use of various forms of falsehood in order to either cover up inadequacies or further self-interests. Like Montaigne, La Rochefoucauld sees any attempt to unmask the "genuine person" (*l'être vrai*) hiding in each individual as an important first step on the road to leading a virtuous life. This concept of *l'être vrai* goes far beyond the idea of sincerity to include a fundamental harmony between the individual's true nature and his or her behavior toward others:

> Wenn La Rochefoucauld von einem Menschen sagte, er sei wahr, so meinte er damit nicht nur die Aufrichtigkeit, wofür das Wort *sincère* ausgereicht hatte, sondern er wollte zum Ausdruck bringen, daß das Verhalten dieses Menschen mit seinem Wesen im Einklang stand. (Frey 391; see Appendix 32)

This combination of lucidity, sincerity, and internal harmony is a rare phenomenon indeed. *L'être vrai* is thus an ideal toward which we must all strive, but one which most of us will never attain, given the illusory nature of the world around us, the unpredictability of human nature, and the elusive character of truth itself.

* * *

Unlike Pascal, who sees truth as unified and indivisible, La Rochefoucauld tends to view truth, both in essence and in the context of human interaction, as heterogeneous and multisided. There is not, as Pascal and his Jansenist colleagues believed, a single Truth of divine origin from which all forms of truth ultimately emanate, but rather a multiplicity of truths that can exist in widely different contexts, without any necessary links, causal or temporal, between them:

> Le vrai, dans quelque sujet qu'il se trouve, ne peut être effacé
> par aucune comparaison d'un autre vrai, et quelque différence
> qui puisse être entre deux sujets, ce qui est vrai dans l'un
> n'efface point ce qui est vrai dans l'autre: ils peuvent avoir
> plus ou moins d'étendue et être plus ou moins éclatants, mais
> ils sont toujours égaux par leur vérité, qui n'est pas plus vérité
> dans le plus grand que dans le plus petit. ("Du vrai," RD
> 183; see Appendix 33)

As Philip Lewis has pointed out, this definition of truth "sharply
divorces the notion from a quantitative sense of completeness,
stressing the *quality* of various truths that makes them equal
in truth" (*La Rochefoucauld: The Art of Abstraction* 147; emphasis mine). For La Rochefoucauld, it is this qualitative aspect of truth that, when applied to human beings and their social
behavior, makes the study of human nature such a challenging
and at the same time fascinating enterprise.

In "Du vrai," La Rochefoucauld goes beyond stressing that
all forms of truth possess this qualitative dimension. At the same
time, he also resolutely contends that all truths are relative. What
is true in one instance is not necessarily true in another. Even
more importantly, perhaps, what makes one individual truthful and sincere does not necessarily make someone else any
more inclined to truthfulness and sincerity. Everything depends
on the circumstances and on the degree to which the truths
involved are appropriate to the situation and to the person or
persons who are hiding or divulging them. Two different situations can easily contain a different number of truths. In other
words, a quantitative difference between them does exist. However, in that they both contain some form of truth, it is not necessarily possible to find a qualitative difference between them:

> Un sujet peut avoir plusieurs vérités, et un autre sujet peut
> n'en avoir qu'une: le sujet qui a plusieurs vérités est d'un
> plus grand prix, et peut briller par des endroits où l'autre
> ne brille pas; mais dans l'endroit où l'un et l'autre est vrai,
> ils brillent également. ("Du vrai," RD 184; see Appen-
> dix 34)

In seventeenth-century France, such a statement was a radical
departure from the traditional and widely accepted view of the

nature of truth. The principle involved has a number of important consequences for La Rochefoucauld's moral and aesthetic ideas, not the least of which is the connection, made by Plato among others, between truth and beauty.

In aesthetic as in moral matters, La Rochefoucauld places particular emphasis on the degree to which an individual's sense of beauty (and therefore the nature of his or her aesthetic sensibility) is appropriate to that individual's character, values, and other subjective reactions to the world of the senses.[5] It is just as obvious to La Rochefoucauld as it was to Plato that truth is the foundation of beauty:

> La vérité est le fondement et la raison de la perfection, et de la beauté; une chose, de quelque nature qu'elle soit, ne saurait être belle, et parfaite, si elle n'est véritablement tout ce qu'elle doit être, et si elle n'a tout ce qu'elle doit avoir. (MS 49; see Appendix 35)

Above all else, both things and people must be capable of realizing their full potential. An object or a person cannot be described as beautiful if that object or person does not embody some form of truth and at the same time both live up to its own potential and fulfill the expectations of the person who is seeking truth and beauty in it.

In his first major book, *Ursprung des deutschen Trauerspiels* (*The Origin of German Tragic Drama*), Walter Benjamin contends that "Einsicht in die platonische Auffassung vom Verhältnis der Wahrheit zur Schönheit . . . ist für die Bestimmung der Wahrheitsbegriffes selbst unersetzlich" (11) ("an understanding of the Platonic view of the relationship between truth and beauty . . . is indispensable to the definition of truth itself"[trans. John Osborne 30–31]), adding that truth is not so much beautiful "an sich *als für den der sie sucht* [emphasis mine]" ("in itself, *as for whosoever seeks it*"). This is precisely how La Rochefoucauld sees the connection between truth and beauty, not as a relationship that exists in the abstract, but rather as one that is dependent on the values and the interests of the person who is seeking truth. Throughout the *Maximes* and the *Réflexions diverses,* this approach to the problem of truth manifests itself in many subtle and, sometimes, barely perceptible ways.

* * *

Once truth has finally been revealed under one of the many masks with which human beings attempt to disguise it, the central problem for La Rochefoucauld becomes how to express this truth, how to describe as accurately as possible both the truth in question and its immediate context, the world of appearances and illusion in which it is to be found. He soon discovered that the *maxime* was ideally suited to this task, since it can express in concrete, definitive, and lasting form the most abstract ideas, giving form and substance to even the most elusive and paradoxical of truths. As Hans-Jost Frey points out in a short essay on the problem of truth in La Rochefoucauld, some of the stylistic resources that the moralist had at his disposal (such as antithesis and his highly original use of the negative *ne . . . que*) enabled him to use the *maxime* form as a means of analyzing both the masks all people wear and the underlying truth they are designed to conceal:

> Die Maxime ist die Entlarvung des Menschen und die Enthüllung seines wahren Wesens. Sie ist meistens zweischichtig und konfrontiert eine Ebene des Scheins mit einer Ebene der Wahrheit . . . (389; see Appendix 36)

Because *maximes* are written in a sort of eternal present, they communicate to the reader a specific truth about human nature that has in a sense been extracted from the web of falsehoods and disguises in which, according to La Rochefoucauld, all such truths are to be found. As the reactions of some of the earliest readers of the *Maximes* clearly indicate, the *maxime* was understood by La Rochefoucauld's contemporaries to be both a form of truth *and* a highly economical and efficient means of expressing that truth.

Having lived in an unstable world in uncertain times, La Rochefoucauld needed, like all great artists, a means of giving form to the truths he had uncovered. He also needed to ensure that the form given to these truths would endure, unlike the life and times that produced them. In La Rochefoucauld's hands, the maxim turned out to be admirably suited to that task. Two hundred years later, another moralist, Friedrich Nietzsche, was to express a similar faith in the durability of the maxim, in its ability to preserve for future generations the all too human truths which the moralist uncovers:

> Eine gute Sentenz ist zu hart für den Zahn der Zeit und wird von allen Jahrtausenden nicht aufgezehrt, obwohl sie jeder Zeit zur Nahrung dient: dadurch ist sie das grosse Paradoxon in der Litteratur, das Unvergängliche inmitten des Wechselnden, die Speise, welche immer geschätzt bleibt, wie das Salz, und niemals, wie selbst dieses, dumm wird. (*Menschliches, Allzumenschliches,* in *Werke* 4.3: 82; see Appendix 37)

Unlike other literary forms, the maxim as a means of expressing eternal truths is subject neither to the whims of readers and critics nor to the vicissitudes of changing literary tastes. The truths it expresses will always withstand the test of time. It is clear that, like La Rochefoucauld, Nietzsche fully understood the power and the durability of the maxim as an instrument in the search for truth and as a means of expressing that truth, however complicated, paradoxical, or disturbing it might be.

Chapter Four

Self-love, Self-interest, Self-deception

> *Quelque découverte que l'on ait faite dans le pays de l'amour-propre, il y reste encore bien des terres inconnues.*
>
> La Rochefoucauld, *Maxime* 3[†]

> *Dieu a permis, pour punir l'homme du péché originel, qu'il se fît un dieu de son amour-propre pour en être tourmenté dans toutes les actions de sa vie.*
>
> La Rochefoucauld, *Maxime posthume* 22[‡]

Just as the theme of truth and falsehood begins and in a sense ends the *Réflexions diverses,* the concept of *amour-propre* is the theme with which the text of the *Maximes* opens and closes. However, *l'amour-propre* is not just the idea that La Rochefoucauld stresses at both the beginning and the end of the *Maximes.* Rather, it is a concept that underlies and informs his entire view of human nature. He sees it as a supremely powerful force functioning as the primary motivator of each individual's actions. It is the ultimate source of all feelings, tastes, and passions, whether people are aware of it or not. According to La Rochefoucauld, it is *amour-propre,* more than any other faculty or motivating force, that consistently, although often unconsciously, thwarts and subverts the human desire for truth.

[†] Whatever discoveries one has made in the realm of self-esteem, many uncharted regions still remain there.

[‡] In order to punish man for original sin, God has allowed him to make a god of his self-love, so that he will be tormented by it throughout his entire life. (CF)

Since individuals' best interests, as determined and defined by their *amour-propre,* are often, for a variety of compelling reasons, inconsistent with their innate need to find the truth, *l'amour-propre* skillfully places endless roadblocks in the path of their search for it. Because self-love plays a role in virtually every aspect of human behavior, it constantly and inevitably comes into conflict with whatever motivating forces tend to push the individual into promoting the cause of truth. Behind the resistance to the desire for truth, behind the often unconscious but nevertheless powerful predilection for falsehood, as behind all other human foibles, lie the fundamental desire for self-preservation and the uncontrollable need for self-aggrandizement exhibited by all, no matter how altruistic their motives may sometimes appear.

In the first *maxime supprimée,* his long and elaborate series of reflections on its nature and function, La Rochefoucauld defines self-love as an all-powerful force that can, and often does, act independently of the will, almost as if it were an autonomous entity capable of deceiving the conscious Self and secretly subverting its day-to-day operations. First and foremost, self-love is an all-encompassing force that effortlessly transforms everything it touches:

> L'amour-propre est l'amour de soi-même, et de toutes choses pour soi; il rend les hommes idolatres d'eux-mêmes, et les rendrait les tyrans des autres si la fortune leur en donnait les moyens; il ne se repose jamais hors de soi, et ne s'arrête dans les sujets étrangers que comme les abeilles sur les fleurs, pour en tirer ce qui lui est propre. (MS 1; see Appendix 38)

Not only does self-love make human beings worship themselves more than all other living creatures but it also directly and profoundly influences the individual's emotional and intellectual responses and reactions to fellow human beings. Above all, it possesses, almost as if it were a totally autonomous force, an insatiable lust for power. An enthusiastic student of history, particularly of contemporary history, La Rochefoucauld, perhaps thinking of Mazarin or the Cardinal de Retz, seems fascinated by the speed with which unbridled self-love can lead to tyranny.

Throughout this remarkable text, La Rochefoucauld uses an elaborate and effective form of personification to analyze the countless strategies and subterfuges that our own self-love conceives and employs in order to exert and preserve its influence over us. There is almost nothing this power-hungry secret agent will not do to ensure its ultimate victory over the other motivating forces existing within each of us and with which it must constantly compete. Although it usually acts like an experienced general, marshaling forces from well behind the line of fire, self-love can, if necessary, go over to the enemy and plot its own destruction:

> Il est dans tous les états de la vie, et dans toutes les conditions; il vit partout, et il vit de tout, il vit de rien; il s'accommode des choses, et de leur privation; il passe même dans le parti des gens qui lui font la guerre, il entre dans leurs desseins; et ce qui est admirable, il se hait lui-même avec eux, il conjure sa perte, il travaille même à sa ruine. Enfin il ne se soucie que d'être, et pourvu qu'il soit, il veut bien être son ennemi. Il ne faut donc pas s'étonner s'il se joint quelquefois à la plus rude austérité, et s'il entre si hardiment en société avec elle pour se détruire, parce que, dans le même temps qu'il se ruine en un endroit, il se rétablit en un autre; quand on pense qu'il quitte son plaisir, il ne fait que le suspendre, ou le changer, et lors même qu'il est vaincu et qu'on croit en être défait, on le retrouve qui triomphe dans sa propre défaite. (MS 1; see Appendix 39)

This apparent desire or willingness to contribute to its own destruction is a clever ruse which self-love occasionally brings into play when it feels particularly vulnerable or open to attack. Such an extraordinary self-defense mechanism enables it to survive even the most prolonged offensive from the opposing forces of altruism. What is extraordinary about this passage is La Rochefoucauld's use of military imagery (war, enemy, victory, defeat) to describe the strategies self-love adopts in its struggle not just with external forces, but also with competing motives and impulses *within the individual's psyche itself.*

Like some of his contemporaries, but in much stronger terms than most, La Rochefoucauld stresses the ability of self-love to penetrate to the innermost recesses of the human soul and the far-reaching and often debilitating effects of the malign influence that such deep penetration allows it to exert.[1] Self-love, he claims, is capable of creating or destroying our most intimate desires, including the will to live and to die:

> Le désir de vivre ou de mourir sont des goûts de l'amour-
> propre dont il ne faut non plus disputer que des goûts de la
> langue ou du choix des couleurs. (Liancourt 243; see Ap-
> pendix 40)

Because the "appetites" of self-love are so subject to change,
even such basic instincts as the life-force and the death wish
are easily activated or suppressed from one moment to the next.
Similarly, what makes human beings act so maliciously toward
each other is not necessarily malice itself. Rather, such behavior is yet another example of the power of self-love:

> Peu de gens sont cruels de cruauté, mais tous les hommes
> sont cruels et inhumains d'amour-propre. (Liancourt 176;
> see Appendix 41)

Since self-love can transform the meekest and least aggressive
person among us into a cruel tyrant, it is no wonder that human beings come into conflict with each other so often and with
such devastating results. The far-reaching political ramifica-
tions of this view of self-love go a long way toward explaining why some of La Rochefoucauld's strongest pronouncements
on the subject of self-love, most of which are to be found in
the Liancourt manuscript, were later omitted or toned down in
the published text of the *Maximes.*

Despite the highly original and strikingly modern elements
to be found in La Rochefoucauld's analysis of the all-encompassing and yet often indiscernible role played by self-love in
the functioning of the human psyche, it must be remembered
that some of what the author of the *Maximes* has to say on the
subject is derived more or less directly from Augustine's concept of *amor sui.* On one level, his concept of self-love should
therefore be seen as an integral part of the distinctly Augustinian dimension of his work.[2] In this respect, La Rochefoucauld
is simply following an important trend in the moral and religious thought of his age. At the same time, it can be demon-
strated that his critical examination of *l'amour-propre* and its
effects goes far beyond studies carried out by either Descartes
or Pascal. Seen from the perspective of the post-Nietzschean
and post-Freudian era, La Rochefoucauld's analyses constitute
a radically new approach to the whole question of psychological motivation.[3] Much more forcefully than any of his contem-

poraries, La Rochefoucauld helped to initiate a long debate on the nature and function of what would today be called egotism. Thanks in part to La Rochefoucauld's provocative statements on the subject, this debate has continued, albeit somewhat sporadically, for over three hundred years.

* * *

In addition to his many definitions and descriptions of self-love itself, La Rochefoucauld takes great pains to explain and differentiate as precisely as possible the other terms that were commonly used in the seventeenth century to describe egotism: *l'intérêt* (self-interest), *l'orgueil* (pride, or as Hobbes and Burton called it, "vain-glory"), and *la fierté* (pride, as it manifests itself externally, in the form of haughtiness, insolence, or snobbery). Unlike many of his contemporaries, La Rochefoucauld sees these terms (and the concepts they refer to) as closely related to each other, but nevertheless quite distinct. Although the definitions he provides for these terms are often based on highly imaginative metaphors and elaborate personifications, he also provides examples that make the differences among the terms much clearer and help the reader gain a better understanding of the various contexts in which he uses them.

Self-interest is the "soul" of self-love, the faculty that gives self-love, among other things, its ability to perceive sensations and to react to them. More importantly, it is not just a series of desires we want to fulfill or objectives we want to attain, but also a paralyzing force that prevents us from reacting to or even being fully aware of the aims, impulses, and concerns of others:

> L'intérêt est l'âme de l'amour-propre, de sorte que, comme le corps, privé de son âme, est sans vue, sans ouïe, sans connaissance, sans sentiment et sans mouvement, de même l'amour-propre séparé, s'il le faut dire ainsi, de son intérêt, ne voit, n'entend, ne sent et ne se remue plus; de là vient qu'un même homme qui court la terre et les mers pour son intérêt devient soudainement paralytique pour l'intérêt des autres; de là vient le soudain assoupissement et cette mort que nous causons à tous ceux à qui nous contons nos affaires; de là vient leur prompte résurrection lorsque dans notre narration nous y mêlons quelque chose qui les regarde; de sorte que nous voyons dans nos conversations et dans nos traités que dans un même moment un homme perd connaissance

> et revient à soi, selon que son propre intérêt s'approche de
> lui ou qu'il s'en retire. (MP 26; see Appendix 42)

In other words, self-interest helps self-love maintain contact
with the outside world, with society, but, paradoxically, at the
same time it prevents self-love from taking any interest what-
soever in anything that will not in some way help it to fulfill
its own needs or to further its own ends. Because we are so
preoccupied with our own concerns, hearing about the problems of others always has a paralyzing effect on our desire to
carry on a conversation with them.

By describing the connection between self-interest and self-love
in this way, La Rochefoucauld gives the term *self-interest* a much
more precise definition than the widely used meaning of "ce
qu'on a affection de conserver ou d'acquérir, ce qui nous importe
soit dans notre personne, soit dans nos biens" ("that which we
want to conserve or acquire, that which is important to us either to our person or to our possessions"). His definition gives
form and substance to the more general meaning of the term:
"tout ce qui regarde le bien, la gloire, le repos, tant de l'Estat
que des particuliers" (Furetière, "Intérêt") ("that which concerns the well-being, the glory, the peace and quiet, of the State
as well as of individuals"). Self-interest for La Rochefoucauld is
not simply the desire to defend and preserve one's interests, to
maintain one's position in society. Rather, it is the means by
which self-love establishes and maintains contact with others,
setting up lines of defense against the outside world. Such an
elaborate strategy, put into practice over long periods of time,
allows self-love to continue to perform its myriad of important functions. In this regard, the *Maximes,* like many moral
treatises of the time, clearly illustrate a major shift in focus
occurring in the second half of the seventeenth century, away
from "le narcissisme auto-idolâtre de la créature, stigmatisé dans
une perspective spirituelle" ("the self-idolizing narcissism of
the creature, stigmatized in a spiritual perspective") toward the
much more modern view of egotism as "l'égocentrisme inté-
ressé, condamné dans une perspective sociale" (Rohou 82) ("self-
interested egocentrism, condemned in a social perspective").
The importance of this shift, for La Rochefoucauld and for
succeeding generations of moralists, cannot be overstated.

The other two terms which La Rochefoucauld uses to describe the fundamental egotism of human beings, *l'orgueil* and *la fierté,* bear somewhat the same relationship to each other as do *l'amour-propre* and *l'intérêt,* in that *l'orgueil* is pride in the sense of an innate predilection to prefer personal interests and achievements over those of a rival, whereas *la fierté* involves the various ways in which that pride manifests itself outwardly and is perceived by others. According to La Rochefoucauld, pride is a universal phenomenon:

> L'orgueil est égal dans tous les hommes, et il n'y a de différence qu'aux moyens et à la manière de le mettre au jour. (M 35; see Appendix 43)

People are all equally proud, he contends, but they do not all display their pride in the same way or to the same degree. From one individual to another, the specific form that pride takes may vary widely. Nevertheless, the outward signs by which human beings manifest their pride all come under the rubric of *la fierté,* which is "the bugle and banner of pride" ("l'éclat et la déclaration de l'orgueil") (MS 6).

* * *

Whether it is called *l'amour-propre* or *l'orgueil,* self-love or pride, egotism is consistently presented in the *Maximes* as an independent force, a Proteus-like magician trained in the use of artifice, constantly changing disguises, taking up and then dropping an almost infinite number of masks. Like the Baroque hero, egotism is a born actor. Only when this maguslike figure temporarily becomes tired of playing so many parts does it begin to reveal its true nature:

> L'orgueil, comme lassé de ses artifices et de ses différentes métamorphoses, après avoir joué tout seul tous les personnages de la comédie humaine, se montre avec un visage naturel, et se découvre par la fierté; de sorte qu'à proprement parler la fierté est l'éclat et la déclaration de l'orgueil. (MS 6; see Appendix 44)

In this *maxime,* La Rochefoucauld describes the activities of *l'orgueil* in eminently Baroque terms. Most of the time, *l'orgueil* is practicing some form of artifice, playing a role, "posing" as something it is not. It is constantly and quite deliberately moving from one form of *artifice* to another. This elaborate process of metamorphosis comes to an end only when *l'orgueil* abandons its disguises and shows its "visage naturel," a strategy intended to deceive like the masks which, up to that point, it has persisted in wearing. The idea that when artifice no longer works, others can still be deceived by unexpectedly displaying complete candor can also be found in Baltasar Gracián's *Oráculo manual y arte de prudencia* (1647), a text that may or may not have directly influenced La Rochefoucauld, but with which the *Maximes* nevertheless have a remarkable number of close affinities:

> Auméntase la simulación al ver alcanzado su artificio, y pretende engañar con la misma verdad. Muda de juego, por mudar de treta, y hace artificio del no artificio, fundando su astucia en la mayor candidez. (155; see Appendix 45)

In La Rochefoucauld, as in Gracián, self-love and pride are the primary sources of artifice and deceit, but by no means the only ones.

In its relations with the outside world, self-love operates under the cover of so many disguises that its true nature is difficult if not impossible to discover. It employs so many sophisticated ruses and depends so heavily on its arsenal of artifices to survive that it is itself often unaware of all the hidden feelings it has generated and all the good or harm it is doing:

> On ne peut sonder la profondeur, ni percer les ténèbres de ses abîmes. Là il est à couvert des yeux les plus pénétrants; il y fait mille insensibles tours et retours. Là il est souvent invisible à lui-même, il y conçoit, il y nourrit, et il y élève, sans le savoir, un grand nombre d'affections et de haines; il en forme de si monstrueuses que, lorsqu'il les a mises au jour, il les méconnaît, ou il ne peut se résoudre à les avouer. (MS 1; see Appendix 46)

Using some of the most remarkably modern imagery in his repertory, La Rochefoucauld describes self-love as living in almost constant darkness, which protects it from attack, but which also causes it to harbor many illusions and misconceptions about its own strengths and weaknesses. It is no wonder that human beings nurture innumerable illusions about themselves, since their own self-love is in itself the source of so many elaborate fictions and deliberate falsehoods:

> De cette nuit qui le couvre naissent les ridicules persuasions qu'il a de lui-même; de là viennent ses erreurs, ses ignorances, ses grossièretés et ses niaiseries sur son sujet; de là vient qu'il croit que ses sentiments sont morts lorsqu'ils ne sont qu'endormis, qu'il s'imagine n'avoir plus envie de courir dès qu'il se repose, et qu'il pense avoir perdu tous les goûts qu'il a rassasiés. Mais cette obscurité épaisse, qui le cache à lui-même, n'empêche pas qu'il ne voie parfaitement ce qui est hors de lui, en quoi il est semblable à nos yeux, qui découvrent tout, et sont aveugles seulement pour eux-mêmes. (MS 1; see Appendix 47)

This quintessentially Baroque "darkness visible" in which self-love lurks and from which it murkily perceives the outside world is, in La Rochefoucauld's view, one of the greatest sources of error and misjudgment that repeatedly plague human beings. What is worse, it prevents them from finding the truth or, once truth has been found, of recognizing it as such.

Throughout the Liancourt manuscript, La Rochefoucauld emphasizes that it is not just the illusion-making properties of self-love that lead to so much deceit and duplicity but also the fact that self-love is constantly transforming both itself and the objects of its affections and hatreds. In other words, not only is reality being disguised or distorted, but the disguises used and the distortions induced are in a constant state of flux:

> Comme si ce n'était pas assez à l'amour-propre d'avoir la vertu de se transformer lui-même, il a encore celle de transformer ses objets; ce qu'il fait d'une manière fort étonnante, car non seulement il les *déguise* si bien qu'il y est lui-même abusé, mais aussi, comme si ses actions étaient des miracles, il change l'état et la nature des choses soudainement . . . (Liancourt 107; emphasis mine; see Appendix 48)

The covert actions of such a talented miracle-worker do more to undermine individuals' hopes of gaining access to the truth, whether it be about themselves or about others, than any other single factor. Both the consummate artfulness and the

remarkable adaptability of self-love make it an extremely difficult obstacle to surmount.

Since La Rochefoucauld so persistently emphasizes self-
love's talent for illusion-making and its taste for disguises of
all kinds, it is not surprising that he also uses the metaphor of
the theater to describe its methods and its machinations.[4] In
seventeenth-century France, the idea of life as a play in which
all people assume roles and frequently impersonate others was
widely used to underscore the illusory nature of much that happens in society. In his writings on society, the chevalier de Méré,
for example, often refers to this most Baroque of metaphors:

> Je suis persuadé qu'en beaucoup d'occasions il n'est pas
> inutile de regarder ce qu'on fait comme une Comédie, et
> de s'imaginer qu'on joue un personnage de théâtre. (*Suite
> du discours du monde* 3: 158; see Appendix 49)

In one of the earliest critical studies of the *Maximes,* Henri de
La Chapelle-Bessé sees the Baroque construct of *theatrum
mundi* as central to La Rochefoucauld's social vision:

> Je les regarde comme des leçons d'un maître qui entend
> parfaitement l'art de connaître les hommes, qui *démêle admi-
> rablement bien tous les rôles qu'ils jouent dans le monde,*
> et qui non seulement nous fait prendre garde aux différents
> caractères des personnages du théâtre, mais encore qui nous
> fait voir, en levant un coin du rideau, que cet amant et ce
> roi de la comédie sont les mêmes acteurs qui font le docteur
> et le bouffon dans la farce. ("Discours de La Chapelle-Bessé,"
> Truchet ed. 281–82; emphasis mine; see Appendix 50)

Not only are all people engaged in role-playing, but the roles
they play are constantly changing. Life in society requires all
its members to be as flexible and as adaptable as a skilled and
experienced actor.

Although the concept of life as theater was commonly used
in La Rochefoucauld's time, the contexts in which the metaphor appears in the *Maximes* differ from those we find in Méré's
Discours or in countless other contemporary works of moral
philosophy, plays, and volumes of poetry. In La Rochefoucauld,
it is not life in general that is implicitly compared to a play,
nor does society form the backdrop for the "human comedy,"

as it often does in Baroque theater. Rather, it is the mental and emotional life of the individual that constitutes the stage upon which consummate actors such as self-love strut about and speak their lines. As Tzvetan Todorov has pointed out, the role-playing that takes place at the level of the psychic activity of every human being is not unlike the *commedia dell'arte,* in which the actors are often deliberately confused with the characters they are playing and one "character" often plays another (37).[5] In this multileveled "human comedy," self-interest and self-love are by far the most versatile actors. They can readily assume any role that circumstances require:

> L'intérêt parle toutes sortes de langues, et joue toutes sortes de personnages, même celui de désintéressé. (M 39; see Appendix 51)

Just as self-love can, when necessary, assume an air of humility and self-mortification, self-interest can, when there is some benefit to be gained, wear the mask of disinterestedness.

* * *

For each of us, the consequences of all this role-playing and willful deceit on the part of our own self-interest and self-love are as pervasive as they are profound. More than any other element in the human psyche, self-love constantly works to destabilize our hearts and minds in subtle ways of which, in many cases, we are scarcely aware:

> Rien n'est si impétueux que ses désirs, rien de si caché que ses desseins, rien de si habile que ses conduites; ses souplesses ne se peuvent représenter, ses transformations passent celles des métamorphoses, et ses raffinements ceux de la chimie. (MS 1; see Appendix 52)

As a result, the judgments we make about ourselves and about others, already highly subjective, become even more so as self-love ingeniously outmaneuvers and in the end completely undermines both our ability to make rational decisions and any tendency we might harbor toward either modesty or altruism.

Over time, the inconstancy and capriciousness of self-love make its scheming and its countless ruses all the more dangerous because the conscious Self can never hope to keep up with the changes wrought both by shifting external circumstances and by the adjustments in strategy and direction that self-love quietly engineers in order to respond to whatever modifications might occur in the outside world. The number and nature of its desires may vary greatly, but self-love is always ready to adapt to change:

> Il a de différentes inclinations selon la diversité des tempéraments qui le tournent, et le dévouent tantôt à la gloire, tantôt aux richesses, et tantôt aux plaisirs; il en change selon le changement de nos âges, de nos fortunes, et de nos expériences; mais il lui est indifférent d'en avoir plusieurs ou de n'en avoir qu'une, parce qu'il se partage en plusieurs et se ramasse en une quand il le faut, et comme il lui plaît. (MS 1; see Appendix 53)

The inherent instability and the ceaseless activity that characterize self-love are best compared, La Rochefoucauld concludes, to that eminently Baroque symbol of mutability, the sea:

> Voilà la peinture de l'amour-propre, dont toute la vie n'est qu'une grande et longue agitation; la mer en est une image sensible, et l'amour-propre trouve dans le flux et le reflux de ses vagues continuelles une fidèle expression de la succession turbulente de ses pensées, et de ses éternels mouvements. (MS 1; see Appendix 54)

Like Proteus, self-love—the god intended to torment humans and punish them for Original Sin—is constantly at work, adapting its form and behavior to its changing needs while at the same time deliberately disguising its true intentions and real objectives.

* * *

One of the most original aspects of La Rochefoucauld's analysis of the processes and functions of self-love and of their paralyzing effect on the individual's search for truth is the way in which he presents a wide range of human emotions and modes of behavior as being ultimately, despite appearances to the contrary, produced or motivated by self-love. However innocent or altruistic some motives may appear, they are nevertheless only false fronts designed to mask the secret workings of self-love. There are, for example, two very different kinds of anger, one of which is more or less innocent, to the extent that anything to do with human behavior toward others is ever really innocent; the other kind is essentially a manifestation of self-love's momentary frustration or fear:

> On ne fait point de distinction dans la colère, bien qu'il y en ait une légère et quasi innocente, qui vient de l'ardeur de la complexion, et une autre très criminelle, qui est à proprement parler la fureur de l'orgueil et de l'amour-propre. (Liancourt 25; see Appendix 55)

As is often the case in La Rochefoucauld, the same outward appearances can be, and often are, easily produced by two completely different causes, one of which is natural and essentially harmless and the other malevolent and perverse. It is precisely this type of phenomenon that makes the work of the moralist so difficult.

Just as anger can stem directly from self-love, so does the suffering we experience at the death of a friend or the misfortunes of others. The words we may use to describe such afflictions are only that, words:

> Quelque prétexte que nous donnions à nos afflictions, ce n'est souvent que l'intérêt et la vanité qui les causent. (M 232; see Appendix 56)

The tears we shed at the death of someone close to us are not really for that person, but for ourselves. In La Rochefoucauld's view, grief is one of our most hypocritical emotions, a form of suffering in which we not only mislead others but also deceive ourselves:

> Il y a dans les afflictions diverses sortes d'hypocrisie. Dans l'une, sous prétexte de pleurer la perte d'une personne qui nous est chère, nous nous pleurons nous-mêmes; nous regrettons la bonne opinion qu'il avait de nous; nous pleurons la diminution de notre bien, de notre plaisir, de notre considération. Ainsi les morts ont l'honneur des larmes qui ne coulent que pour les vivants. Je dis que c'est une espèce d'hypocrisie, à cause que dans ces sortes d'afflictions *on se trompe soi-même*. (M 233; emphasis mine; see Appendix 57)

Once again, our own self-interest and self-love force us to mask the true motives of our actions by fabricating false ones. As is often the case, we are as much the victims of the deceit being practiced as are our fellow mourners.

Similarly, the joy we experience at the good fortune of others is almost never sincere, since in such instances we are, as usual, being driven by self-love. However real our joy may seem, it is a product of self-interest, not of any sincere feelings we might have for others:

> Le premier mouvement de joie que nous avons du bonheur de nos amis ne vient ni de la bonté de notre naturel, ni de l'amitié que nous avons pour eux; c'est un effet de l'amour-propre qui nous flatte de l'espérance d'être heureux à notre tour, ou de retirer quelque utilité de leur bonne fortune. (MS 17; see Appendix 58)

Here, the true nature of our motives is perhaps somewhat more apparent to us than in the case of grief, but we are still not fully conscious of the role selfishness plays behind the scenes. The joy we feel at the good luck or success of others is really only a premonition of the satisfaction we will derive from being lucky or successful ourselves, or from finding some means of turning their good fortune to our own advantage.

The loyalty we show toward others may appear, by its very nature, to be rooted in altruism, but in the Liancourt manuscript La Rochefoucauld ascribes even an act of fidelity to the secret *trafics*[6] ("dealings") of self-love. When it appears that we are being faithful to others, we are really only trying to put ourselves in a position from which we can exert even greater power and influence over them:

> La fidélité est une invention rare de l'amour-propre par laquelle l'homme, s'érigeant en dépositaire des choses précieuses, se rend lui-même infiniment précieux; *de tous les trafics de l'amour-propre* c'est celui où il fait moins d'avances et de plus grands profits; c'est un raffinement de sa politique, car il engage les hommes par leurs biens, par leur honneur, par leur liberté et par leur vie qu'ils sont forcés de confier en quelques occasions, à élever l'homme fidèle au-dessus de tout le monde. (Liancourt 90; emphasis mine; see Appendix 59)

Self-love, it seems, has an almost infinite capacity for seeing chances to further its own interests and for seizing these opportunities to camouflage its real intentions. Very often, the qualities we most admire in ourselves and in others are nothing more than the "inventions" of self-love.

Even such a seemingly altruistic quality as magnanimity, which La Rochefoucauld's contemporaries associated with courage and the other distinguishing characteristics of great men, is presented in the *Maximes* as an "invention" of self-love, as nothing more than a clever ruse by which pride attempts to exert its power and influence over the individual. Once the efforts pride makes to bring him or her to a state of complete self-control have been successful, the individual is ready to gain control of others:

> La magnanimité est un noble effort de l'orgueil par lequel
> il rend l'homme maître de lui-même pour le rendre maître
> de toutes choses. (MS 51; see Appendix 60)

Once again, self-love has been able to satisfy its never-ending need for power by exerting its influence in a subtle but very effective manner. At the same time, it has once again succeeded in hiding its subversive activities under the guise of a "noble" gesture.

Nowhere in the realm of human behavior does self-love play a more important role, of course, than in love and jealousy. As Marcel Proust was to demonstrate many years later in *A la recherche du temps perdu,* jealousy has very little to do with the love one individual feels for another, and everything to do with the love of self:

> Il y a dans la jalousie plus d'amour-propre que d'amour. (M
> 324; see Appendix 61)

In La Rochefoucauld, this underlying egotism, which spawns jealousy and which is at the root of all forms of love, manifests itself in a variety of ways. Why, for example, do lovers like to spend so much time talking to each other? It is not because they like each other's company, but rather because such amorous encounters provide each of them with an unequaled opportunity to discuss their favorite topic:

> Ce qui fait que les amants et les maîtresses ne s'ennuient
> point d'être ensemble, c'est qu'ils parlent toujours d'eux-
> mêmes. (M 312; see Appendix 62)

In the anonymous English translation of the *Maximes* that ap-
peared in London in 1694, the translator chose to present this
idea in a very different way:

> The reason why *Ladies* are easie in one anothers company,
> is because they never talk of any thing but themselves. (*Moral
> Maxims and Reflections* 312; emphasis in original)

This rather dubious translation does not convey the idea, quite
clear in the original, that the maxim applies equally to both sexes.
In what is in other respects a reasonably good translation, La
Rochefoucauld's attitude toward women has been made to appear misogynistic, when in fact, in this instance at least, he
portrays the two sexes as being equal.

* * *

In addition to their ability to destabilize our mental and emotional lives and to create a multiplicity of masks in order to
disguise their true identities and to camouflage their real objectives, self-love and pride can also perform another important function: blinding us to our own shortcomings by preventing
us from understanding what really motivates our actions and
reactions. As Jean Starobinski was the first to contend, La
Rochefoucauld's theories about self-love and self-interest appear on the surface to be very simple. Cutting through the veil
of appearances to reveal the "genuine person" underneath is
merely a question of showing "la présence d'une passion
unique—l'amour-propre—derrière ses innombrables déguise-
ments" ("Complexité" 33) ("the presence of a single passion—
self-love—behind its innumerable disguises"). It is precisely
this aspect of La Rochefoucauld's thought that first attracted
the attention of Jacques Lacan, who, in the second series of
his famous "seminars," expressed surprise at the way in which
La Rochefoucauld's theory of *amour-propre* was viewed by
many of the moralist's contemporaries:

> Il est curieux que cela ait paru si scandaleux, car que disait-
> il? Il mettait l'accent sur ceci, que même nos activités en

apparence les plus désintéressées sont faites par souci de la gloire, même l'amour-passion ou l'exercice le plus secret de la vertu.[7] (Lacan, "Psychologie et métapsychologie" 17–18; see Appendix 63)

Lacan's reading of the *Maximes* will be discussed in greater detail in a later chapter of this study. What is interesting in the present context is the emphasis Lacan places on the fundamental principle to which La Rochefoucauld returns again and again, the extent to which we are blind to the forces that motivate us.

With a depth and subtlety of analysis Lacan was to greatly admire, La Rochefoucauld points out, however, that the power of self-love to make us lose sight of our faults and misinterpret our own motivations can, when and if the situation warrants it, be redirected. Most of the time, pride prevents us from seeing our shortcomings:

L'aveuglement des hommes est le plus dangereux effet de leur orgueil: il sert à le nourrir et à l'augmenter, et nous ôte la connaissance des remèdes qui pourraient soulager nos misères et nous guérir de nos défauts. (MS 19; see Appendix 64)

However, when we run the risk of seeing our faults exposed to the scrutiny of others, self-love can instantaneously alter its course and enable us, momentarily at least, to see our faults more clearly, and so disguise them more effectively:

Ce qui fait voir que les hommes connaissent mieux leurs fautes qu'on ne pense, c'est qu'ils n'ont jamais tort quand on les entend parler de leur conduite: le même amour-propre qui les aveugle d'ordinaire les éclaire alors, et leur donne des vues si justes qu'il leur fait supprimer ou déguiser les moindres choses qui peuvent être condamnées. (M 494; see Appendix 65)

Paradoxically, no blinding force is as deceptive as one that on rare occasions allows us to see clearly. But then of all human faculties, none is as unstable, as unreliable, and as unrelenting as self-love.

Chapter Five

A Theory of the Passions

Il y a dans le cœur humain une génération per-
pétuelle de passions, en sorte que la ruine de l'une
est presque toujours l'établissement d'une autre.
La Rochefoucauld, *Maxime* 10[†]

Quelque soin que l'on prenne de couvrir ses
passions par des apparences de piété et d'honneur,
elles paraissent toujours au travers de ces voiles.
La Rochefoucauld, *Maxime* 12[‡]

Throughout his writings, La Rochefoucauld portrays self-love
as only one of the many passions that originate in the perpetual
"movements" of the human heart and help to keep the "soul"
of the afflicted individual in a state of continual agitation and
uncertainty. According to La Rochefoucauld, the multitude of
wants and desires that are generated in all of us, randomly and
in rapid succession, throughout our lives inevitably produce
major obstacles in our search for truth, both about ourselves
and about others, in a way that is disturbingly similar to the
subtle subterfuges of self-love. In the seventeenth century, most
moralists believed that the passions are caused by the motion
or "agitation" that initially occurs in the blood as a reaction to
external stimuli.[1] The word *mouvement* refers both to "the principle of warmth which conserves life in all animate bodies"
(in other words, the so-called movements of the blood) and,
figuratively, to the moral and spiritual "movements" which

[†] In the human heart there is an endless procreation of passions: as
soon as one is dethroned, another almost always comes to power.

[‡] However carefully we disguise our passions to look like piety and
honor, the mask proves of no avail.

57

directly affect the emotional life of every human being (Furetière, "Mouvement"). By contending that the human heart is constantly undergoing such "movements," La Rochefoucauld once again stresses the underlying instability of the human psyche.

Furthermore, this "endless procreation of passions" takes place without our knowledge or consent; the speed at which one desire diminishes in intensity or is extinguished completely is determined by circumstances that are entirely beyond our control. Whether a given emotion such as love or ambition rages within us for a month or for several years depends not on decisions made by the conscious Self or on any rational principle but on the nature of the passion itself as well as on a large number of other totally unpredictable factors:

> La durée de nos passions ne dépend pas plus de nous que la durée de notre vie. (M 5; see Appendix 66)

As a consequence, the extent to which our passions can inhibit our ability to discover the truth about ourselves and about others is greatly increased. Since we have no effective means of predicting the length of time a given emotion will exert its power over us, we also cannot begin to assess how great an impact it will have on our attempts to gain access to the truth. For example, the act of falling in or out of love, like the contracting of a disease, cannot be predetermined, because it is the result of a process over which we have no control:

> La plus juste comparaison qu'on puisse faire de l'amour, c'est celle de la fièvre; nous n'avons non plus de pouvoir sur l'un que sur l'autre, soit pour sa violence ou pour sa durée. (MS 59; see Appendix 67)

La Rochefoucauld is not the first writer to use illness as metaphor, but his approach to the topic is an original one. Love resembles sickness, not just, he argues, at the level of the physical symptoms it induces, but also in terms of the powerlessness of its victim to resist infection and the impossibility of predicting the long-term effects it produces. It is no coincidence that this concept of the nature of passion manifests itself in Mme de La Fayette's *La Princesse de Clèves* (1678), in which, for example, the King's desire for Diane de Poitiers survives for over twenty years or Mme de Tournon's love for Sancerre diminishes in intensity over a period of a few months for all kinds of reasons that have nothing to do with either the exercise of their will or the power wielded by their other passions.

Like Pascal, but for very different reasons, La Rochefoucauld portrays human beings as the helpless victims of their passions, defenseless prisoners who can neither withstand the pressure being exerted by these forces nor find the strength to evade their tremendous power. In one of his most pessimistic maxims, La Rochefoucauld suggests that we are as unhappy laboring under the influence of our passions as we are when struggling to free ourselves from their control:

> L'homme est si misérable que, tournant toutes ses conduites à satisfaire ses passions, il gémit incessamment sous leur tyrannie; il ne peut supporter ni leur violence ni celle qu'il faut qu'il se fasse pour s'affranchir de leur joug; il trouve du dégoût non seulement dans ses vices, mais encore dans leurs remèdes, et ne peut s'accommoder ni des chagrins de ses maladies ni du travail de sa guérison. (MP 21; see Appendix 68)

The overwhelming, "tyrannical" power exerted over us by our passions leaves us in such a state of weakness and insensitivity that we easily become even less lucid than we would otherwise be. Although La Rochefoucauld rarely uses the term *lucide,* he sees the consequences of what the Jansenists call the "weaknesses" of man in terms of a tragic loss of lucidity. Moreover, he believes very strongly that all the energy we expend in finding ways to satisfy our desires or to escape from their "fury" could be put to much better use were we able to bring it to bear on the search for truth.

Unfortunately, our passions do much more than simply divert our attention from acquiring knowledge about ourselves and the world. Like self-love, they mislead and deceive us in innumerable and often very subtle ways. They carry out this deception both by hiding from us their true identity and by preventing us from perceiving—and thus perhaps avoiding—the many follies and transgressions into which they never fail to lead us:

> Il s'en faut bien que nous connaissions tout ce que nos passions nous font faire. (M 460; see Appendix 69)

Because we are not even aware of the extent to which our emotions rule our lives, we consistently fail to understand both the motives and the consequences of many of our actions. When we think we are acting out of charity or a sense of responsibility toward others, for example, we may be unconsciously trying to satisfy our lust or our envy, our greed or our ambition. Since one of the first effects that our passions produce is a temporary suspension of our ability to reason, they are able to rule our lives completely, often forcing us to do many things we would never otherwise dream of doing.

Unlike Descartes, whose *Traité des passions de l'âme* (*Treatise on the Passions of the Soul,* 1649) was widely read in La Rochefoucauld's time, the author of the *Maximes* has little faith in human ability to withstand the onslaught of the emotions. In a letter to Princess Elisabeth, dated 15 September 1645, Descartes suggests that the extent to which we are deceived by our passions can be regulated—or at least to some degree influenced—by the exercise of the will:

> Ce que nous devons soigneusement remarquer, afin que, lorsque nous nous sentons émus de quelque passion, nous suspendions notre jugement, jusques à ce qu'elle soit apaisée; et que nous ne nous laissions pas aisément tromper par la fausse apparence des biens de ce monde. (608–09; see Appendix 70)

In this letter, and elsewhere, Descartes expresses considerable optimism regarding the human ability to suspend and later to re-activate judgment, to mitigate the effects of the passions through a conscious effort to resist their fury. In La Rochefoucauld, such valiant attempts at self-control are a complete waste of time, since we are very often not even aware that some newly generated passion is at work within us. In any case, even if we were to try to limit its power, another, perhaps even more powerful, passion would immediately begin to take hold of us.

In his belief that our passions are one of the greatest obstacles we encounter in our search for truth, La Rochefoucauld is much closer to the Jansenist thinker Pierre Nicole, who sees humans as too weak and too corrupt to control their passions. Like the *Maximes,* Nicole's *Essais de morale* (*Essays on Morals*) frequently allude to human beings' inability to distinguish between truth and falsehood once they have fallen victim to their passions:

> Quand un homme a le cœur corrompu, toutes les vérités qu'il connoît deviennent les instrumens de ses passions: et bien loin de lui être utiles pour faire le bien, elles ne lui servent qu'à colorer le mal qu'il fait, et à faciliter l'exécution de ses mauvais desseins. (3: 203; see Appendix 71)

La Rochefoucauld rarely uses a term such as "corrompu," but in other respects this passage is very close to both the tone and the substance of many of his most memorable maxims. Despite these similarities, the two moralists are still far apart with respect to both their presuppositions and their objectives. Nicole's reasons for analyzing how practical everyday truths come to be transformed into the "instruments" of the passions are very different from La Rochefoucauld's. The Port-Royal writer's analysis is clearly intended to show that humanity is in desperate need of God, whereas the metaphysical underpinnings of La Rochefoucauld's theory of the passions are much less clear.

* * *

One of the reasons our passions are so likely to lead us into error and seduce us with falsehoods of many kinds is that not only do they resemble self-love in their power to deceive us but also that they are very often the direct result of the machinations of that tyrannical illusion-maker. In essence, La Rochefoucauld claims, our passions are the products of the likes and dislikes, of the whims and fancies, of our own self-love:

> Les passions ne sont que les divers goûts de l'amour propre.
> (MP 28; see Appendix 72)

Because our self-love is such a profoundly unstable force, the passions it helps to create and destroy cannot be otherwise. Nowhere is this more evident than in the case of *l'amour-passion*. When we are in love, many of our actions are motivated only by our instinct for survival coupled with our eternal need to further our own interests:

> Il n'y a point de passion où l'amour de soi-même règne si puissamment que dans l'amour; et on est toujours plus disposé à sacrifier le repos de ce qu'on aime qu'à perdre le sien. (M 262; see Appendix 73)

Rather than enabling us to achieve a higher degree of self-aware-ness and to understand more fully our innermost impulses and desires, love is one of the most important sources of illusions and falsehoods. Ultimately, there is no escape. "Wir sind aus Liebe," Nietzsche complains two centuries later in *Morgenröthe* (*Daybreak*), "arge Verbrecher an der Wahrheit . . ." ("For the sake of love, we are inveterate transgressors against truth . . .").[2]

Because La Rochefoucauld's views on the role self-love plays in love and most other passions run counter to the more tradi-tional concept of love that held sway before, during, and after his time, they have caught the attention of his readers at least as much as some of his other, seemingly more radical, ideas. La Rochefoucauld's influence in this area has been profound. The eighteenth-century French moralist Vauvenargues, for ex-ample, may well be echoing La Rochefoucauld when he makes the following observations in his own *Réflexions et maximes:*

> Tous les ridicules des hommes ne caractérisent qu'un seul vice, qui est la vanité; et, comme les passions des gens du monde sont subordonnées à ce faible, c'est, apparemment, la raison pourquoi il y a si peu de vérité dans leurs manières, dans leurs mœurs, et dans leurs plaisirs. La vanité est ce qu'il y a de plus naturel dans les hommes, et ce qui les fait sortir le plus souvent de la nature.[3] (2: 440; see Appendix 74)

In this passage, Vauvenargues uses the term *vérité* with pre-cisely the same meaning as La Rochefoucauld does. For him, as for the author of the *Maximes,* the concept of truth is closely connected to the idea of genuineness, of authenticity. Both of them would agree that one of our biggest problems is that we find far too many reasons for forgetting to be genuine, for al-lowing *l'être vrai* to be disguised or even totally abandoned, simply because we are at the mercy of our passions. Long be-fore Freud and modern psychoanalysis, humans were viewed as creatures so driven by desire that they are willing to sacri-fice anything that might impede their pursuit of pleasure.

* * *

In the seventeenth century, the term *passion* covered a much wider range of human feelings and emotions than it does today. In the age of Louis XIV, it could refer not just to passions, such as love or anger, which manifest themselves in a highly visible and sometimes even violent manner, but also to much less dramatic and dynamic forms of desire, such as fear and boredom.[4] In a remarkable series of *maximes,* La Rochefoucauld thus analyzes the pervasive influence and the tremendous power indolence or laziness (*la paresse*) can exert over our other passions and our lives in general. Since it sets out to destroy our other passions and to prevent us from trying to reach the objects of our desires, *la paresse* is, paradoxically, one of the most powerful forces that deter us from understanding our own desires and, more importantly, from learning the truth about our own motivations and those of others. In some ways, it is almost as great an obstacle in the search for truth as self-love itself.

Although it does its work quietly and often imperceptibly, indolence, like self-love, has the power to transform our lives completely:

> C'est se tromper que de croire qu'il n'y ait que les violentes passions, comme l'ambition et l'amour, qui puissent triompher des autres. La paresse, toute languissante qu'elle est, ne laisse pas d'en être souvent la maîtresse; elle usurpe sur tous les desseins et sur toutes les actions de la vie; elle y détruit et y consume insensiblement les passions et les vertus. (M 266; see Appendix 75)

In the never-ending war which our passions wage against each other, indolence often manages, despite its passivity and apparent lack of energy, to overcome all its rivals and determine the course of both our emotional and our spiritual lives. Following La Rochefoucauld's lead, Furetière defines *la paresse* as "un vice moral" ("a moral vice") that prevents us from doing our duty[5] and seriously inhibits us from gaining reliable knowledge about ourselves.

What makes indolence so dangerous, La Rochefoucauld cautions, is that we are not even aware of all the aspects of our lives affected by it. We do not know much about how any of our passions function. We know less about indolence than about most of the others. Of all our passions,

> elle est la plus ardente et la plus maligne de toutes, quoi-
> que sa violence soit insensible, et que les dommages qu'elle
> cause soient très cachés; si nous considérons attentivement
> son pouvoir, nous verrons qu'elle se rend en toutes rencontres
> maîtresse de nos sentiments, de nos intérêts et de nos plaisirs;
> c'est la rémore qui a la force d'arrêter les plus grands vais-
> seaux, c'est une bonace plus dangereuse aux plus importantes
> affaires que les écueils, et que les plus grandes tempêtes; le
> repos de la paresse est un charme secret de l'âme qui sus-
> pend soudainement les plus ardentes poursuites et les plus
> opiniâtres résolutions; pour donner enfin la véritable idée
> de cette passion, il faut dire que la paresse est comme une
> béatitude de l'âme, qui la console de toutes ses pertes, et
> qui lui tient lieu de tous les biens. (MS 54; see Appendix 76)

Paradoxically, indolence is both a powerful "force for harm" and a source of consolation, of "beatitude" that soothes the soul and further masks the profound effects such a malignant power can have on our already turbulent and troubled lives. Once again and in very striking terms, La Rochefoucauld portrays the inner life of individuals as a battleground on which opposing forces create conflicts and tensions that cannot easily be resolved. Indolence is a more dangerous emotion than most because, like self-love, it disguises both its methods and its objectives.

Like all our other passions, indolence deprives us of our freedom to act according to the dictates of our will or our conscience.[6] It has a neutralizing effect on our willingness to act decisively and on our innate sense of right and wrong. In one of his most enigmatic pronouncements on the subject, La Rochefoucauld suggests, in the Liancourt manuscript, ironically, that the devil himself may have played a role in establishing indolence as a major power over human actions:

> Il semble que c'est le diable qui a tout exprès placé la paresse
> sur la frontière de plusieurs vertus. (Liancourt 209; see
> Appendix 77)

The precarious position that indolence occupies with respect to the virtues may well explain why it is capable of providing consolation to a troubled soul while at the same time depriving that individual of moral freedom. Such paradoxes are a fundamental characteristic of human nature. They help to explain why we are such complicated and unpredictable creatures.

* * *

According to La Rochefoucauld, all of our passions can also have positive effects on us, despite their ability to confuse and lead us into errors as well as falsehoods of many kinds. Unlike most other moralists of his time, he believes that some emotions can inspire us to do great things and even, under the right circumstances, lead us into living more, not less, virtuous lives. In his self-portrait, the "Portrait de M. R. D. par lui-même," he states this view very clearly:

> J'approuve extrêmement les belles passions: elles marquent la grandeur de l'âme, et quoique dans les inquiétudes qu'elles donnent il y ait quelque chose de contraire à la sévère sagesse, elles s'accommodent si bien d'ailleurs avec la plus austère vertu que je crois qu'on ne les saurait condamner avec justice. (Truchet ed. 257–58; see Appendix 78)

It could be argued that in making this statement La Rochefoucauld is looking at the question not as a moralist, but rather as an old soldier or, like the chevalier de Méré, as a *mondain* interested only in the practical art of pleasing others. The fact that not all desires are necessarily destructive makes the complex interplay of our evolving passions all the more deceptive and destabilizing.

In his "Discours des agrémens," Méré argues that if we were able to divest ourselves of our passions completely, life would be both boring and useless. Furthermore,

> ce sont principalement les passions qui font exceller les meilleurs ouvriers. Car quand on le veut ardemment, on en cherche les plus seurs moyens. Et c'est par ce grand soin qu'on se rend habile en tout ce qu'on entreprend. (2: 49; see Appendix 79)

In other words, the emotions can have a purely utilitarian function that consists of bringing forth and displaying our hidden talents. In the *Maximes,* La Rochefoucauld makes precisely the same argument. Paradoxically, the passions can, under some circumstances, make us more lucid and more resourceful than we would otherwise be. In this case, as in so many other situations, we are often totally unaware of our own potential, just as we are usually unaware of our own weaknesses:

> Il semble que la nature ait caché dans le fond de notre esprit des talents et une habileté que nous ne connaissons pas; les passions seules ont le droit de les mettre au jour, et de nous donner quelquefois des vues plus certaines et plus achevées que l'art ne saurait faire. (M 404; see Appendix 80)

The discovery of these hidden talents contributes to our self-knowledge, but unfortunately only in a very limited and usually short-lived way. It is a measure of the fundamental instability of human existence (*l'inconstance,* in Baroque terms) that the same passion has the power either to blind us completely or to help us achieve a greater degree of lucidity.

* * *

As we have seen, La Rochefoucauld's theory of the passions provides us with a complex if sometimes contradictory analysis of how our wants and desires are produced and of the various ways in which they help to determine many aspects of our daily lives. At one level, he seems to believe that they have purely physical causes, that, for example, they can be awakened by changes in the temperature of the blood:

> Toutes les passions ne sont autre chose que les divers degrés de la chaleur, et de la froideur, du sang. (MS 2; see Appendix 81)

His greatest contributions to the theory of the passions lie, however, in the close connections he sees between them and self-love and in his careful demonstration of the ways in which they can misdirect and ultimately completely subvert our attempts to gain greater self-knowledge as well as knowledge of the secret desires and private emotions that motivate our friends.

Because of their instability, our own passions are constantly changing both in degree and in nature, making the task of analyzing and understanding them virtually impossible. At the same time, they systematically undermine our judgment by making us both reject those truths that are likely to hinder our passionate pursuits and foster the falsehoods that tend to favor or expedite them.[7] As Dyke puts it in *The Mystery of Selfe-deceiving,* "many wholesome truths have been distasted, onely by reason of the prejudice which our naughty affections have conceived against the teachers . . ." (282). In some cases, La Rochefoucauld claims, this rejection of truth in favor of falsehood takes place against our will. In other instances, however, we quite consciously choose to cover up the true nature of our passion, either in order to satisfy our desire more easily or because we are ashamed of having succumbed to it and therefore prefer to disguise it as something else.

Whatever Descartes and his disciples may have said to the contrary, we do not have the ability to resist the power of our passions. When we are under the malign influence of one of our many emotions, our behavior toward others may seem to result from a process of conscious decision-making, but, La Rochefoucauld concludes, this is almost never the case. Even the most lucid and logical human beings inevitably fall prey to the errors and illusions to which their passions make them prone. Our love of truth is a powerful force, but it is not as powerful as the self-centered pleasure we derive from satisfying our wants and desires. Vauvenargues, who often disagrees with much that La Rochefoucauld has to say about self-love, is in total agreement with the author of the *Maximes* concerning the disastrous effect our passions can have on our desire for truth:

> L'indifférence où nous sommes pour la vérité dans la morale vient de ce que nous sommes décidés à suivre nos passions, quoi qu'il en puisse être; et c'est ce qui fait que nous n'hésitons pas lorsqu'il faut agir, malgré l'incertitude de nos opinions. Peu importe, disent les hommes, de savoir où est la vérité, sachant où est le plaisir. (2: 435; see Appendix 82)

This is a question that would lead Vauvenargues and his contemporaries in other directions, but it also probably represents a good example of the profound influence La Rochefoucauld exerted on the thought of the eighteenth century and later.

Chapter Six

Vices and Virtues

*Nos vertus ne sont, le plus souvent, que des vices
déguisés.*

Exergue[†]

*Ce qui nous empêche souvent de bien juger des
sentences qui prouvent la fausseté des vertus,
c'est que nous croyons trop aisément qu'elles sont
véritables en nous.*

La Rochefoucauld, *Maxime posthume* 7[‡]

In La Rochefoucauld's moral system, there is little doubt that
true virtue, like true friendship and true love, does exist, but
like many other human qualities and attributes, it rarely exists
in a pure form. What we usually consider to be virtue is either
merely the appearance of virtue or else virtue that is intricately
and inextricably bound up with vice. From his close association with Jacques Esprit, the author of *De la fausseté des vertus
humaines* (*Of the Falsity of Human Virtues,* 1678),[1] and no doubt
also as a direct result of his own personal experience, La Rochefoucauld acquired the firmly held conviction that almost all our
so-called virtues are false, partly because of their very nature
and partly because of the conscious and deliberate attempts that
all human beings routinely make to cover up their baser instincts with the mask of virtue. In either case, our desire to
uncover the true motives of others or, for that matter, to gain a

---

[†] Our virtues are mostly disguised vices.

[‡] We are often prevented from truly appreciating aphorisms which
disprove the purity of the virtues by our eagerness to believe that in our
own case, at least, these are quite unalloyed. (CF)

greater understanding of our own is vastly outweighed by our inability both to differentiate the appearance of virtue from virtue itself and to distinguish virtue from vice.

In a direct reference to Guarini's *Il pastor fido* (*The Faithful Shepherd,* 1589), La Rochefoucauld claims that all our virtues are the product of artifice and deceit rather than our essential goodness or sense of honor, that what we try to pass off as virtue is almost always a false front and a sham:

> On peut dire de toutes nos vertus ce qu'un poète italien a dit de l'honnêteté des femmes, que ce n'est souvent autre chose qu'un art de paraître honnête. (MS 33; see Appendix 83)

Whether it be courtly virtue or chastity, whether it be intellectual virtues or the so-called cardinal virtues,[2] what passes for virtue in society very often stems from a carefully orchestrated campaign of feigned emotion and hypocritical behavior carried out by those we believe to be virtuous. This elaborate system of ruses serves to camouflage the true nature of their motives. Regardless of the circumstances, almost all so-called virtues are used to hide a very different reality from that which appears on the surface.

* * *

What makes matters much worse, for those who seek truth in this world of constantly misleading appearances and carefully disguised motives, is the fact that all of us are continually falling victim to one vice[3] after another. In just the same way that we find ourselves escaping the malign influence of one passion, only to be caught up immediately in another, we find ourselves subject to vice after vice after vice. Unfortunately, there is very little we can do to avoid succumbing to each of them in turn:

> On peut dire que les vices nous attendent dans le cours de la vie comme des hôtes chez qui il faut successivement loger; et je doute que l'expérience nous les fît éviter s'il nous était permis de faire deux fois le même chemin. (M 191; see Appendix 84)

In the course of an individual's life, he or she will inevitably be exposed to various vices. Even considerable experience in life will not necessarily either lessen the risk of exposure or increase the chances of a swift recovery from the symptoms produced. Moreover, the fact that we continue to "journey" from one vice to another unfortunately does not preclude our being assailed and corrupted by several different vices at the same time:

> Ce qui nous empêche souvent de nous abandonner à un seul vice est que nous en avons plusieurs. (M 195; see Appendix 85)

Not only do vices overcome our resistance in rapid succession but we are also often simultaneously under the influence of several different vices, all of which play some part, at one time or another, in destabilizing our emotions and in preventing us from achieving any meaningful degree of self-knowledge.

Because of the highly unstable nature of our desires and motivations, the interrelationships between our vices and whatever opposing or complementary virtues we may have are continually changing as we grow older and as the circumstances in which we find ourselves evolve. Whether we refer to these changing circumstances as chance (*le hasard*) or fortune, it is clearly they, and not our conscious selves, which determine the present and future course of both our virtues and our vices:

> La fortune fait paraître nos vertus et nos vices, comme la lumière fait paraître les objets. (M 380; see Appendix 86)

We are being naive, La Rochefoucauld cautions, if we think that we can exert any meaningful degree of influence or control over our vices or alleviate in any way either their immediate or their long-term consequences. We may think that we can overcome or somehow attenuate the profound effects our vices are having on us, but this is only an illusion:

> Quand les vices nous quittent, nous nous flattons de la créance que c'est nous qui les quittons. (M 192; see Appendix 87)

In this case, as in so many others, we are the victims of forces beyond our control and which we are very often at a loss even to comprehend, let alone to find the strength to combat. Like many other forces within us, our vices seriously compromise our ability to understand our own motivations. For the same reason, those of others remain even more elusive.

* * *

At the beginning of the *Maximes,* La Rochefoucauld stresses that our vices resemble our virtues to such an extent and on so many different levels that "[n]os vertus ne sont, le plus souvent, que des vices déguisés" (exergue) ("our virtues are mostly disguised vices"). The idea that the distinction between vice and virtue can, and often does, become so blurred that it tends to disappear almost entirely was vigorously debated by moralists of many different persuasions throughout the seventeenth century. In *The Mystery of Selfe-deceiving,* for example, Dyke contends that

> our pur-blinde hearts, deceived with that shadow of resemblance, which Vice sometimes carrieth of Vertue, doe oftentimes embrace and receive grosse vices, in stead of glorious vertues. (182)

In other words, the reason we "embrace" vice so readily is not necessarily because we are tainted with Original Sin, but because our "hearts" are deceived by the close if superficial similarity between vice and virtue. A decade later, in the preface to his *Principes de la philosophie* (*Principles of Philosophy,* 1647), Descartes takes up this issue of the similarity between vice and virtue, contending that while some vices may have the appearance of virtue, there is nevertheless a great deal of difference between true virtues and those which, although they appear to be virtues, are really vices:

> Il y a beaucoup de différence entre les vraies vertus et celles qui ne sont qu'apparentes; et il y en a aussi beaucoup entre les vraies qui procèdent d'une exacte connaissance de la vérité, et celles qui sont accompagnées d'ignorance ou d'erreur. Les vertus que je nomme apparentes ne sont, à proprement parler, que des vices, qui, n'étant pas si fréquents

que d'autres vices qui leur sont contraires, ont coutume d'être plus estimés que les vertus qui consistent en la médiocrité, dont ces vices opposés sont les excès.[4] (See Appendix 88)

Like La Rochefoucauld, Descartes sees a close and important connection between the problem of virtues and vices and the question of truth. Descartes, however, has much more faith in man's ability to overcome the obstacles that the existence of apparent or "superficial" virtues places in the path of those who seek "an exact knowledge of the truth."

La Rochefoucauld goes much further than his predecessors in stressing the close similarities that virtues can have to their corresponding vices and in pointing out the ways in which these similarities help to blur the distinction between virtue and vice. As a result, we are regularly prevented from clearly differentiating between the two, either with respect to the actions of others or with respect to our own. Vices, La Rochefoucauld reminds us, are a *necessary* element in the composition of virtues:

> Les vices entrent dans la composition des vertus comme les poisons entrent dans la composition des remèdes. La prudence les assemble et les tempère, et elle s'en sert utilement contre les maux de la vie. (M 182; see Appendix 89)

Once prudence has completed its task, this meticulously blended mixture of vices and virtues may make the hardships of life easier to bear, but it also makes identifying and emulating virtue in its purest form ultimately impossible, since virtue is almost always intertwined with vice.[5]

Many readers of La Rochefoucauld have interpreted his theory of vices and virtues as an attempt to undermine the concept of virtue or, at the very least, to promote the cause of vice by claiming that all our virtues are contaminated to some degree by vices. But, as Henri de La Chapelle-Bessé astutely observed, La Rochefoucauld's real objective is to show that all our actions result from a complex blend of both vice and virtue, truth and falsehood. Of the various criticisms which could be made of the *Maximes,*

> [i]l me semble que la première est celle-ci: *que les Réflexions détruisent toutes les vertus* [emphasis in original]. On peut

> dire à cela que l'intention de celui qui les a écrites paraît
> fort éloignée de les vouloir détruire; il prétend seulement
> faire voir qu'il n'y en a presque point de pures dans le monde,
> et que dans la plupart de nos actions il y a *un mélange
> d'erreur et de vérité, de perfection et d'imperfection, de vice
> et de vertu* [emphasis mine] . . . ("Discours de La Chapelle-
> Bessé," Truchet ed. 271–72; see Appendix 90)

If one accepts this argument, it becomes clear that moral decisions involve much more than a simple question of choosing
between right and wrong, of deciding whether to exercise virtue or to practice vice. As Nietzsche very clearly perceived in
the early 1870s, La Rochefoucauld is one of the first moralists
to formulate a theory of morality not based on rational decision-making but rather that takes into account the complex and
often contradictory nature of basic human impulses and drives.[6]
The confusion and uncertainty created by the intertwining of
vices and virtues make the task of finding the real motives behind all our actions much more complicated than most of La
Rochefoucauld's contemporaries were willing to admit.

* * *

Just as the life of the passions is regulated to a large extent by
self-love, the exercise of virtue and the practice of vice are
strongly influenced by the ever-present persuasive power of
vanity and self-interest. However powerful either our virtuous
instincts or our inclinations toward vice may be, they are always tempered or exacerbated by purely selfish motives. In the
end, vanity has the power to neutralize if not to destroy all our
virtues:

> Si la vanité ne renverse pas entièrement les vertus, du moins
> elle les ébranle toutes. (M 388; see Appendix 91)

If our virtues and our self-interest conflict, as they often do, it
is our virtues that quickly give way before the rising tide of
self-interest:

> Les vertus se perdent dans l'intérêt, comme les fleuves se
> perdent dans la mer. (M 171; see Appendix 92)

This very striking image emphasizes, among other things, how close virtue and self-interest are to each other and how difficult it is to delineate the border between them. The speed with which our virtuous instincts are subverted and our moral values weakened by self-interest leaves us in a state of doubt and confusion, in which the distinction between truth and falsehood becomes increasingly difficult to make.

In the Liancourt manuscript, La Rochefoucauld makes it quite clear that it is our selfishness and pride, our conscious or unconscious devotion to our own self-interest, that ultimately prevent us from distinguishing vice from virtue. It is not just that what appears to be virtue very often is not, but also that our pride and self-love tend to dress up vices as virtues:

> Nous sommes préoccupés de telle sorte en notre faveur que ce que nous prenons le plus souvent pour des vertus ne sont en effet que des vices qui leur ressemblent, *et que l'orgueil et l'amour-propre nous ont déguisés.* (Liancourt 3; emphasis mine; see Appendix 93)

In this instance as in so many others, self-love and self-interest serve as powerful blinding forces that totally mislead us and, as a result, effectively prevent us from accurately diagnosing our own ills. Vices and virtues do resemble each other in many ways, as Dyke observed, but we are much more likely to be taken in by the apparent similarities between the two if the resulting confusion is likely to somehow further our own selfish interests.

Furthermore, the public pronouncements we make about our own vices and virtues and about those of others are also determined and conditioned by self-interest to a much greater degree than by any overriding sense of morality or concern for our fellow human beings. Like so many other words circulating in society and which moralists expend so much energy in attempting to define, virtue and vice are often only empty words that our self-interest prompts us to invoke in order to cover up its questionable tactics and secret maneuvers:

> Le nom de la vertu sert à l'intérêt aussi utilement que les vices. (M 187; see Appendix 94)

If we either complain loudly about the vices other people engage in or express our admiration for their acts of virtue, we are very likely not acting out of moral indignation or following long-established ethical principles, but simply responding to the dictates of our own self-interest:

> On ne blâme le vice et on ne loue la vertu que par intérêt.
> (MS 28; see Appendix 95)

At the same time as we delude ourselves into thinking that we are making sound moral judgments, we also delude others into believing that we can indeed distinguish vice from virtue. As La Rochefoucauld emphasizes again and again, what really concerns us is not whether we or someone else is truly virtuous or not, but rather what others will think both of our own conduct and of the judgments we make publicly about that of others.

* * *

If for some reason self-love is not at work behind the scenes attempting to disguise vice as virtue, then one of our many other passions will eagerly step in to perform the same function. In one of his most pessimistic statements on the subject, La Rochefoucauld claims that what passes for virtue is merely an illusion created by our passions in order to mask the true nature of our basest desires. As long as we give the vice in question a respectable name, we can do whatever we want:

> Ce que le monde nomme vertu n'est d'ordinaire qu'un fantôme formé par nos passions, à qui on donne un nom honnête, pour faire impunément ce qu'on veut. (MS 34; see Appendix 96)

The moral nihilism to which this concept of virtue seems to lead La Rochefoucauld was strongly condemned by many subsequent generations of French moralists, and yet it resurfaces in many eighteenth-century works, not the least important of which is Laclos's *Les Liaisons dangereuses* (*Dangerous Liaisons,* 1782). From the perspective of the late twentieth century, what is perhaps most significant about La Rochefoucauld's theory of virtue and vice is the fact that in society the use of the word *virtue* is far more important than the reality behind it.

La Rochefoucauld's concerted attack on the self-centered and often hypocritical motives that wear the mask of virtue can of course be viewed in various contexts and interpreted in various ways. First, as La Rochefoucauld implies in a letter addressed to Père Thomas Esprit, the brother of Jacques, in February 1664, his objective in writing the *Maximes* was the same as that of Jacques. Both moralists, he claims, sought to prove

> que la vertu des anciens philosophes païens . . . a été établie sur de faux fondements, et que l'homme, tout persuadé qu'il est de son mérite, n'a en soi que *des apparences trompeuses de vertu* dont il éblouit les autres et dont souvent il se trompe lui-même . . .[7] (Truchet ed. 578; emphasis mine; see Appendix 97)

Undoubtedly, the concept of virtue he promulgated in the *Maximes* is first and foremost an attack on the classical concept of *virtu* and on what La Rochefoucauld sees as the false principles underlying the philosophies of Seneca and of many other thinkers of classical antiquity, including no doubt his illustrious predecessor in the art of the aphorism, Marcus Aurelius.

Second, La Rochefoucauld's theory of vice and virtue is also a break with a much more recent past, the "courtly" tradition that runs from Castiglione's *Il Cortegiano* (*The Book of the Courtier,* 1528) to the works of Faret and of other French theoreticians of the courtly virtues.[8] In La Rochefoucauld's eyes, most of the so-called courtly virtues are really masks that cover over a multitude of self-serving and essentially vile motives. In this context, it is quite clear that in attacking social virtues La Rochefoucauld breaks with the values of his class.[9] His ideal is not the perfect courtier, nor the perfect subject of the King, but rather the *honnête homme,* the perfect citizen. One has only to look at what he has to say about heroism and the other aristocratic values such as courage to see how far La Rochefoucauld has strayed from the traditional attitudes and prejudices of his class.

Third, La Rochefoucauld goes on to explore and analyze the consequences of the existence of all these false virtues for social intercourse and for the preservation of social harmony. How can society continue to function, he asks in the *Réflexions diverses,* if its members are constantly deluding themselves and each other with what is only the appearance, the "shadow," of virtue, while at the same time each individual seeks to further his own interests at the expense of everyone else? For La Rochefoucauld, this is one of the fundamental problems human beings must solve if they are to continue to live in a highly organized society and to maintain some degree of social harmony. The solution to this problem, proposed by La Rochefoucauld in "De la société" ("Of Society") and elsewhere in the *Réflexions,* will be discussed in our next two chapters.

Chapter Seven

Disguising the Truth from Others

*Dans toutes les professions chacun affecte une
mine et un extérieur pour paraître ce qu'il veut
qu'on le croie. Ainsi on peut dire que le monde
n'est composé que de mines.*
                La Rochefoucauld, *Maxime* 256[†]

*Il ne faut pas s'offenser que les autres nous
cachent la vérité puisque nous nous la cachons si
souvent nous-mêmes.*
                La Rochefoucauld, *Maxime posthume* 11[‡]

For many writers of the Baroque period, the idea that social
life is founded primarily if not exclusively upon artifice and
illusion was a fundamental principle upon which all attempts
to analyze or satirize the foibles and follies of the social being
were necessarily based. In Gracián's extraordinarily rich and
eminently Baroque novel *El criticón* (*The Critic,* 1651), for
example, the seventh "crisi" of Part I, entitled "La fuente de
los engaños" ("The Fountain [source] of Deceptions"), intro-
duces the reader to the allegorical figure of el Engaño (Deceit),
whose powers are limitless and whose innumerable ruses and
superbly executed subversive tactics make it virtually impossible for human beings engaged in social intercourse to distinguish truth from falsehood to any meaningful degree (*Obras
completas* 574–86). Although he is much less interested in social

---

[†] On all occasions we assume the look and appearance we want to
be known for, so that the world in general is a congregation of masks.

[‡] We should not be resentful when others hide the truth from us, since
we so often conceal it from ourselves. (CF)

satire than Gracián, and much less inclined to express his views of society in purely allegorical terms, La Rochefoucauld nevertheless bases his own social theories on the same underlying principle: the idea that life in society is predicated on the necessity of seeming to be what one is not. In a world where *le paraître* is of much greater importance than *l'être,* the social being experiences a basic need to disguise the truth about himself or herself from others. This uncontrollable need is satisfied by wearing whatever masks are necessary in order to deceive others successfully and thereby to achieve his or her goals in society.

The notion that the efficient functioning of society and the continuing happiness of its members depend directly on a complex process of mutual deceit is a common theme in the work of many seventeenth-century moralists. "We must take notice of the corruption of our hearts," warns Dyke, using a tone often heard in the sermons of the time, "whereby we are ready to deceive our brethren, what by feigning, what by dissembling"(33). The element in La Rochefoucauld's views on the subject that makes them original—and, one could argue, at the same time very modern—is the important set of connections he sees between the act of deceiving others and the sometimes deliberate—and yet often at least partly unconscious—act of deceiving ourselves. The process works both ways. Since we are all deceiving ourselves at one level or another, it is hardly surprising that we are more than ready to deceive others as well. In high society in particular, success and even mere survival depend on our ability to hide our true feelings and to present to the outside world the "look and appearance" needed to create the appropriate illusion. According to La Rochefoucauld, this principle applies to all walks of life, not just to courtiers and ministers of the Crown, nor to one's friends and lovers.[1]

On the question of the many links that exist between the act of deceiving others and the act of deceiving oneself, La Rochefoucauld sets himself apart from his predecessors and outdoes his contemporaries by emphasizing the extent to which our attempts to hide our true character or motives from others tend to lead us, in many cases against our will and often without our realizing what is happening, into disguising them from ourselves as well:

Nous sommes si accoutumés à nous déguiser aux autres
qu'enfin nous nous déguisons à nous-mêmes. (M 119; see
Appendix 98)

In the *réflexion* "De la société," La Rochefoucauld contends
that the strong and persistent human inclination to hide behind
some form of mask, some "look and appearance we want to
be known for," has its origins in a deep-seated desire not to
allow others to see us as we really are. The social being always has some reason, sometimes valid but more often not,
for preferring to present to the world a face and a persona that
are not his or her own:

Comme on doit garder des distances pour voir les objets, il
en faut garder aussi pour la société: chacun a son point de
vue, d'où il veut être regardé; on a raison, le plus souvent,
de ne vouloir pas être éclairé de trop près, et *il n'y a presque
point d'homme qui veuille, en toutes choses, se laisser voir
tel qu'il est.* (RD 188; emphasis mine; see Appendix 99)

This fundamental human desire to be seen from a distance, rather
than from close up, where our weaknesses and our faults are
much more visible, explains why the social being instinctively
sets up a vast array of false fronts and impenetrable lines of
defense. This is an aspect of human nature that has profound
consequences both for the individual and for society as a whole.

The social being wears an assortment of different masks for
two reasons: first, in an attempt at disguise of one sort or another, and second, for the purpose of presenting an exterior, a
"look and appearance," that is not genuine and that is intended
for some specific use. Since all members of society indulge
simultaneously and indiscriminately in this elaborate role-playing exercise, it becomes increasingly difficult to ascertain and
assess the true motives of others. Even the most lucid among
us are easily taken in by the "dissembling" carried out by others. At the same time, we are more than willing to believe the
flattering things others say about us and to accept as truth the
lies and distortions they are putting forth, both about themselves
and about us. Nietzsche echoes this point in *Morgenröthe:*

Wir sind wie Schauläden, in denen wir selber unsere ange-
blichen Eigenschaften, welche Andere uns zusprechen,

> fortwährend anordnen, verdecken oder in's Licht stellen,—
> um uns zu betrügen. (*Werke* 5.1: 251; see Appendix 100)

Social intercourse is thus, in La Rochefoucauld's eyes—and Nietzsche would agree—a vast system in which lies and untruths of various kinds are formulated and exchanged on a regular basis. In such a system, self-deceit and the act of deceiving others continue to operate in a reciprocal and self-perpetuating relationship. Although other moralists of the period, notably La Bruyère, also portray social life as based on deceit and the exchange of lies, only La Rochefoucauld attempted to study in depth the complex relationship between the psychological and social dimensions of the problem.

* * *

When embarking on a career in society, La Rochefoucauld points out, it is particularly important to wear the appropriate mask, to ensure that one presents to the world the right "look and appearance" from the very beginning. Society tends to reward appearances rather than reality. Typically, it is always appearances that impress and influence others, regardless of how worthy the underlying reality might be. In the Liancourt manuscript, La Rochefoucauld explains that society systematically rewards the appearances of excellence rather than real merit simply because in most cases none of its members know or understand what the latter is:

> Le monde, ne connaissant point le véritable mérite, n'a garde de pouvoir le récompenser; aussi n'élève-t-il à ses grandeurs et à ses dignités que des personnes qui ont de belles qualités apparentes et il couronne généralement tout ce qui luit quoique tout ce qui luit ne soit pas de l'or. (Liancourt 165; see Appendix 101)

In another maxim from the same version of the text, La Rochefoucauld again underscores, with what can only be described as a great deal of bitterness, how successful one can be in society if only one knows how to make the most of one's qualities, no matter how limited, inadequate, or inappropriate:

> On admire tout ce qui éblouit, et l'art de savoir bien mettre en œuvre de médiocres qualités dérobe l'estime et donne

souvent plus de réputation que le véritable mérite. (Liancourt 185; see Appendix 102)

Again, the gold metaphor emphasizes the importance of the purely visual impact of an individual's qualities, mediocre as they may be. It is the fact that the material shines which counts, not what it really is or what it contains. The qualities an individual possesses are less important than the uses to which they are put, the skill with which they are displayed, and the extent to which their exhibition succeeds in producing the desired effect.

Throughout the various versions of the *Maximes* can be found the idea that *real* merit is rarely recognized in society because most people exhibit only its external trappings and not the quality itself ("le véritable mérite"). Like the Liancourt manuscript, the definitive text of the *Maximes* emphasizes the vital importance of appearances:

Le monde récompense plus souvent les apparences du mérite que le mérite même. (M 166; see Appendix 103)

The consequences of this state of affairs are immediate and far-reaching. If society rewards the mere appearance of merit, and not merit itself, its members have no choice but to display only those qualities society is willing to recognize and reward, and to cover up or suppress those which are ultimately of no practical use in social intercourse. La Rochefoucauld was not the only moralist of his time to understand this aspect of the society in which he lived, but he was the first to formulate in such precise and eloquent terms this fundamental social law.

So pervasive is the perception that life in society is a question of appearances rather than reality, of artifice rather than substance, that even establishing a name for oneself in society requires dissembling and deceit rather than talent, merit, or a willingness to work hard. As soon as they begin to make a mark for themselves in society—and perhaps even before—individuals must realize the importance of *appearing* to have already made that mark:

Pour s'établir dans le monde, on fait tout ce que l'on peut pour y paraître établi. (M 56; see Appendix 104)

Throughout his career as soldier and courtier, La Rochefoucauld had no doubt seen countless examples of this kind of role-playing and deceit and of the success with which such a strategy often met. In the *Maximes,* he tried to present a coherent and thorough analysis of the basic human traits that predispose the social being to behave in almost all circumstances as though life were simply a long and continuous masked ball.[2]

* * *

In a wider context, for La Rochefoucauld all human activity in society, beginning with childhood and the earliest stages of what we would call today the process of socialization, is based entirely on imitation and affectation. Children possess an air of naturalness and authenticity that they will eventually lose as they gain greater experience of the world. Gradually, they will come to realize that there are other modes of behavior than those they display naturally and without pretense:

> Ce qui fait que la plupart des petits enfants plaisent, c'est qu'ils sont encore renfermés dans cet air et dans ces manières que la nature leur a donnés, et qu'ils n'en connaissent point d'autres. Ils les changent et les corrompent quand ils sortent de l'enfance: ils croient qu'il faut imiter ce qu'ils voient faire aux autres, et ils ne le peuvent parfaitement imiter; il y a toujours quelque chose de *faux* et d'incertain dans cette imitation. Ils n'ont rien de fixe dans leurs manières ni dans leurs sentiments; au lieu d'être en effet ce qu'ils veulent paraître, ils cherchent à paraître ce qu'ils ne sont pas. ("De l'air et des manières," RD 189; emphasis mine; see Appendix 105)

La Rochefoucauld concludes that it is this apparently innate and very powerful urge to imitate that lies at the root of most of society's problems. If we were not so inclined to imitate the manner and behavior of others, we would not contribute so willingly to the multiplicity of errors and illusions that the act of imitation inevitably engenders.

In a social context, the compulsion to seem to be what one is not, to take on an identity that is not one's own, creates a host of problems that La Rochefoucauld believes are caused both by the failure to follow the dictates of the individual's own feelings or instincts and by necessarily unsuccessful attempts to live by the prescriptions of others. In social life, as in art, there are no good copies:

> Chacun veut être un autre, et n'être plus ce qu'il est: ils cherchent une contenance hors d'eux-mêmes, et un autre esprit que le leur; ils prennent des tons et des manières au hasard; ils en font l'expérience sur eux, sans considérer que ce qui convient à quelques-uns ne convient pas à tout le monde, qu'il n'y a point de règle générale pour les tons et pour les manières, et qu'il n'y a point de bonnes copies. (RD 189; see Appendix 106)

When we try to copy the ways of others, we make two very important mistakes: first, we readily imitate others for the sake of imitating them. We do this instinctively, without realizing the extent to which this unconscious imitation takes place. Second, we do not understand that the manner, the tone, and the gestures of others may suit them perfectly, but do not necessarily suit us at all:

> Deux hommes néanmoins peuvent avoir du rapport en plusieurs choses sans être copie l'un de l'autre, si chacun suit son naturel; mais personne presque ne le suit entièrement. On aime à imiter; on imite souvent, même sans s'en apercevoir, et on néglige ses propres biens pour des biens étrangers, qui d'ordinaire ne nous conviennent pas. (RD 189; see Appendix 107)

The affectation and falsity resulting from this need to imitate affect our relations with everyone we meet and with society as a whole. Their effects are compounded by our vanity and self-love, which, as we have seen, always thrive on artifice and falsehoods of all kinds.

In social situations, this deeply ingrained predilection for imitation and affectation, combined with the subtle but powerful motivation provided by self-love, can bring about some extraordinary and paradoxical behavior on the part of an individual driven both by self-interest and by the need to sham and to pose. In most instances, as we have seen, self-love is a blinding force, but when combined with the human penchant for disguise, it can paradoxically provide individuals with great insight into their own weaknesses, enabling them to find the means of preventing others from seeing the truth:

> Ce qui fait voir que les hommes connaissent mieux leurs fautes qu'on ne pense, c'est qu'ils n'ont jamais tort quand on les entend parler de leur conduite: le même amour-propre qui les aveugle d'ordinaire les éclaire alors, et leur donne des vues si justes qu'il leur fait supprimer ou déguiser les moindres choses qui peuvent être condamnées. (M 494; see Appendix 108)

Human nature being what it is, however, self-love sometimes forces people into thinking that they have too few faults, in which case, instead of affecting a degree of virtue and perfection they have never attained, the penchant of individuals for affectation will cause them to imitate, and eventually to acquire, faults that they previously never had:

> Il semble que les hommes ne se trouvent pas assez de défauts; ils en augmentent encore le nombre par de certaines qualités singulières dont ils affectent de se parer, et ils les cultivent avec tant de soin qu'elles deviennent à la fin des défauts naturels, qu'il ne dépend plus d'eux de corriger. (M 493; see Appendix 109)

In *Les Caractères* (*The Characters*), La Bruyère provides a number of highly amusing examples of this kind of studied affectation, but for La Rochefoucauld, the process of acquiring faults through imitation and affectation has serious and long-lasting consequences. Such strange and paradoxical behavior on the part of the social being makes the task of distinguishing between reality and affectation, between truth and falsehood, even more difficult and frustrating than it would otherwise be.

* * *

Since human beings, once they have entered society and have seen how it works, tend both to disguise their true motives and to affect false ones, the task of discovering the real motives behind what appears to be virtuous or altruistic behavior on the part of others becomes a long and arduous one. Some of La Rochefoucauld's most valuable and enduring insights into human nature involve the process of disguising base and purely self-centered motives as universally recognized virtues. Ultimately, even our most altruistic impulses are only a means of disguising our attempts to satisfy our self-love or our envy, our lust or our ambition:

> Nous aurions souvent honte de nos plus belles actions si le monde voyait tous les motifs qui les produisent. (M 409; see Appendix 110)

The task of the moralist, as La Rochefoucauld conceived and practiced it, is to look behind the veil of appearances, to unmask the passions and the prejudices being disguised as positive moral values. A whole range of attitudes and qualities traditionally associated with a strong sense of morality, even with the concept of Christian virtue, are revealed in the *Maximes* as mere cover or camouflage for much baser instincts.

Moderation or temperance, for example, a virtue prized by the Ancients as well as by many of La Rochefoucauld's contemporaries, is actually a defense mechanism, an ostentation, or an unjustified and totally inappropriate feeling of self-importance. Depending on one's situation in society and the extent and origins of one's good fortune, a modest or temperate reaction to success can be explained in various ways:

> La modération est une crainte de tomber dans l'envie et dans le mépris que méritent ceux qui s'enivrent de leur bonheur; c'est une vaine ostentation de la force de notre esprit; et enfin la modération des hommes dans leur plus haute élévation est un désir de paraître plus grands que leur fortune. (M 18; see Appendix 111)

In this instance, La Rochefoucauld is clearly distancing himself from the Baroque. Ostentation, often a positive and useful activity in Baroque literature, is seen here as motivated by fear and insecurity rather than by a legitimate and sincere desire to display one's talents or virtues. Far from exhibiting restraint or exercising caution in such situations, La Rochefoucauld argues, most people react in a self-centered and self-protective manner, by attempting to avoid at all costs the censure of others and by taking extraordinary measures in order to make themselves *appear* to be something they are not.

In his "definition" of humility, traditionally one of the most important Christian virtues, La Rochefoucauld combines several of his favorite themes in a way that leaves little room for the exercise of Christian moral values. Disguise and deceit motivated by self-love and the lust for power are the real driving forces that operate under the mask of humility:

> L'humilité n'est souvent qu'une feinte soumission, dont on se sert pour soumettre les autres; c'est un artifice de l'orgueil qui s'abaisse pour s'élever; et bien qu'il se transforme en mille manières, il n'est jamais mieux déguisé et plus capable de tromper que lorsqu'il se cache sous la figure de l'humilité. (M 254; see Appendix 112)

This brutal definition of humility is couched in language that is Baroque both in origin and in tone. Indeed, what could be more Baroque than a process that combines artifice, disguise, and metamorphosis? In this case, as in so many others, human behavior is secretly determined and directed by self-love, and the result is an attempt to deceive others through artifice and the skillful manipulation of appearances. This is "often" what happens, but not always.

If true humility in the Christian sense does exist, La Rochefoucauld claims in another maxim, it can be, somewhat paradoxically, the mark of Christian virtue. Without it, he concludes, we would simply continue to live with all our faults:

> L'humilité est la véritable preuve des vertus chrétiennes: sans elle nous conservons tous nos défauts, et ils sont seulement couverts par l'orgueil qui les cache aux autres, et souvent à nous-mêmes. (M 358; see Appendix 113)

True humility, rare as it may be, is the only force capable of liberating us from the power of pride, which, as we have seen, is the overriding principle governing our lives and manipulating us into concealing the truth.

Just as humility is "often" not at all what it seems, most people are not really grateful for the benefits or the good fortune that they owe to the efforts of their friends. Gratitude, in most people, is not a warm feeling of indebtedness to others, a desire to reciprocate by returning a favor or somehow rewarding those who have come to their aid. Rather, it is a means of masking their desire for the continuation of the help, support, or praise they are receiving from others:

> La reconnaissance de la plupart des hommes n'est qu'une
> secrète envie de recevoir de plus grands bienfaits. (M 298;
> see Appendix 114)

This maxim illustrates the extent to which La Rochefoucauld is able to express a profound human truth clearly and succinctly through the use of the negative *ne . . . que.* Genuine gratitude may well exist, in some instances, but the form most often seen in social situations is merely a clever disguise for either unbridled and uncompromising selfishness or an unlimited and unceasing need for self-gratification.

It is hardly surprising that essentially the same process of masking one's true motives in order either to gain an advantage or to avoid suffering defeat frequently takes place in political life as well as in society at large. La Rochefoucauld's view of the reality behind most people's love of justice is expressed in one of his most frequently quoted maxims:

> L'amour de la justice n'est en la plupart des hommes que la
> crainte de souffrir l'injustice. (M 78; see Appendix 115)

In a maxim that was quite understandably omitted from the definitive edition of his text, La Rochefoucauld analyzes what he sees as the true motive behind most people's sense of justice: the instinct for self-preservation. Addressing an issue hotly debated in seventeenth-century Europe, he suggests that the deep-seated fear at the root of our sense of justice is what holds society together and prevents warring factions within society from tearing each other apart:

> La justice n'est qu'une vive appréhension qu'on ne nous ôte
> ce qui nous appartient; de là vient cette considération et ce
> respect pour tous les intérêts du prochain, et cette scrupuleuse
> application à ne lui faire aucun préjudice; cette crainte retient
> l'homme dans les bornes des biens que la naissance, ou la
> fortune, lui ont donnés, et sans cette crainte il ferait des
> courses continuelles sur les autres. (MS 14; see Appendix 116)

As we shall see, La Rochefoucauld does not use the term *social contract,* but a number of his opinions regarding the functioning of society implicitly refer to the concept,[3] even if it is neither formulated in precise terms nor placed in the much wider context in which the political philosophers of the Enlightenment would later seek to define it.

Rulers are not exempt from this widespread tendency to mask true motives with false virtues. Indeed, the power that absolute monarchs possess enables them to practice systematic falsification with impunity. Clemency, for example, can often be merely a "State-trick" designed to win over the populace:

> La clémence des princes n'est souvent qu'une politique pour
> gagner l'affection des peuples. (M 15; see Appendix 117)

In addition, absolute power tends to make the social being's essential falsity infinitely more dangerous in that it allows monarchs to manipulate their subjects much more easily than would otherwise be possible. As a consequence, the merit or the value to society of those who benefit from royal favors such as government posts and pensions is routinely determined in an arbitrary and misleading manner:

> Les rois font des hommes comme des pièces de monnaie;
> ils les font valoir ce qu'ils veulent, et l'on est forcé de les
> recevoir selon leur cours, et non pas selon leur véritable prix.
> (MS 67; see Appendix 118)

In such cases, seeming to be what one is not becomes an integral part of the political process. Like many other aspects of life in society, the world of politics is not just a world of illusions. It is also fundamentally unstable. Just as coins of the realm can be arbitrarily devalued at a moment's notice, or lose their value overnight, political appointees, from ministers and *surintendants* to minor officials, can be demoted or dismissed from one day to the next, as the fall of Nicolas Fouquet had recently and dramatically illustrated.

* * *

Given human beings' propensity for affectation and dissimulation, not to mention the infinitely varied techniques they

employ in order to disguise the truth from others, it seems un-
likely that La Rochefoucauld could envisage any circumstances
under which they might be willing to reveal to others the genuine
person, *l'être vrai,* hiding behind one of the thousand masks
they normally present to the world. Although there may be
"almost no one" who wants to be seen as he or she really is
under all circumstances, La Rochefoucauld does recognize the
possibility that some rare individuals might want to be much
more forthright and honest about their true character, feelings,
and motivation. There can be little doubt, he believes, that

> Nous gagnerions plus de nous laisser voir tels que nous
> sommes, que d'essayer de paraître ce que nous ne sommes
> pas. (M 457; see Appendix 119)

Frankness and candor do exist in some people, but unfortunately
sincerity, which La Rochefoucauld sees as the key to the establishment and survival of a stable society, is a rare phenomenon indeed.

What passes for sincerity in society, in most cases, is a clever
ruse carried out to gain the confidence of others by misleading them into thinking that the false sincerity being displayed
is genuine:

> La sincérité est une ouverture de cœur. On la trouve en fort
> peu de gens; et celle que l'on voit d'ordinaire n'est qu'une
> fine dissimulation pour attirer la confiance des autres. (M 62;
> see Appendix 120)

Rather than trying to insinuate ourselves into the confidence
of others, what we should be doing is opening our hearts, divulging to the world our true identity, without trying either to
mask our faults or to affect traits of character we do not possess.[4]

In the *réflexion* entitled "De la confiance" ("Of Confidence"),
La Rochefoucauld analyzes in detail the connections he sees
between the concept of sincerity and the concept of confidence:

> Bien que la sincérité et la confiance aient du rapport, elles
> sont néanmoins différentes en plusieurs choses: la sincérité
> est une ouverture de cœur, qui nous montre tels que nous
> sommes; *c'est un amour de la vérité,* une répugnance à se
> déguiser, un désir de se dédommager de ses défauts, et de

les diminuer même par le mérite de les avouer. (RD 194;
emphasis mine; see Appendix 121)

In this definition of sincerity, we find all of the elements that
La Rochefoucauld associates with the concept of *l'être vrai:* a
reluctance to indulge in the elaborate process of disguise and
deceit, a willingness to admit one's faults and, above all, a love
of truth. Human beings are by nature false and deceitful, but
this essential falsity and deceitfulness can be overcome if those
who are capable of being sincere are willing to devote suffi-
cient energy to the task. Only those whose love of truth out-
weighs and out balances their predilection for falsity can be
considered sincere.

The truly sincere person, according to La Rochefoucauld's
definition, is one who not only loves truth but is also willing
to act at all times and under all circumstances in a manner that
actively promotes the cause of truth. Sincerity involves always
representing oneself in an honest and truthful manner, particularly when practicing the art of conversation. When speaking
to others about oneself,

> On doit ne leur rien cacher de ce qui ne regarde que nous,
> se montrer à eux toujours *vrais* dans nos bonnes qualités et
> dans nos défauts même, sans exagérer les unes et sans dimi-
> nuer les autres, se faire une loi de ne leur faire jamais de
> demi-confidences; elles embarrassent toujours ceux qui les
> font, et ne contentent presque jamais ceux qui les reçoivent:
> on leur donne des lumières confuses de ce qu'on veut cacher,
> on augmente leur curiosité, on les met en droit d'en vouloir
> savoir davantage, et ils se croient en liberté de disposer de
> ce qu'ils ont pénétré. Il est plus sûr et plus honnête de ne
> leur rien dire que de se taire quand on a commencé de parler.
> ("De la confiance," RD 195–96; emphasis mine; see Ap-
> pendix 122)

It is clear that sincerity is much more than the attitude and demeanor of *l'être vrai,* more than the natural behavior of those
who love truth so much that they are able to surmount the powerful forces continually pushing them in the direction of disguise and deceit. It is also the basis of a whole code of behavior,
a set of rules for surviving and ultimately achieving success
in society.

This understanding of sincerity is closely related to La Rochefoucauld's belief, as outlined in "De l'air et des manières" ("Of Looks and of Manners"), that every individual has "un air," a look or demeanor, that is both natural and peculiar to him or her, and that should never be dropped in order to take on a look or demeanor belonging to another. Rather than trying to assume the "airs" of others, each should try to develop and perfect his or her own, as this is the only way in which *l'être vrai* can remain true to self:

> Il y a un air qui convient à la figure et aux talents de chaque personne; on perd toujours quand on le quitte pour en prendre un autre. Il faut essayer de connaître celui qui nous est naturel, n'en point sortir, et le perfectionner autant qu'il nous est possible. (RD 188; see Appendix 123)

Sincerity or genuineness thus is important in what one says, in how one treats others, and even in the image one projects. It is more of an ideal than an objective, for not even a few very special people could ever hope to realize such a goal.[5]

* * *

In the closely related concepts of sincerity and confidence, La Rochefoucauld sees the basis for all forms of human interpersonal relationships, from personal friendship to complex social organization. Sincerity on the part of others, particularly if it is sustained and practiced consistently, leads us to have confidence in our friends and, on a much larger scale, in the other members of the society in which we live. Such well-founded confidence in others can counteract, or at least attenuate considerably, the friction and divisiveness brought about by the opposing demands of the parties concerned, whether the conflict be between two friends or among the members of society as a whole. In all circumstances involving the interaction of individuals, self-interest plays a vital role:

> Ce que les hommes ont nommé amitié n'est qu'une société, qu'un ménagement réciproque d'intérêts, et qu'un échange de bons offices; ce n'est enfin qu'un commerce où l'amour-propre se propose toujours quelque chose à gagner. (M 83; see Appendix 124)

This mutual adjustment of conflicting interests ("un ménage-ment réciproque d'intérêts") is not an easy undertaking and must be carried out, La Rochefoucauld believes, with great care and sensitivity to the needs of others.

It is the confidence we have in the sincerity and good will of others that enables us to adjust our own requirements to accommodate those of others and to exchange with them the favors and services upon which both a solid friendship and a stable society depend. Making such adjustments means, of course, giving up some of our personal freedom. It is not easy for most human beings to see their own interests mixed up with those of others:

> La confiance ne nous laisse pas tant de liberté, ses règles sont plus étroites, elle demande plus de prudence et de retenue, et nous ne sommes pas toujours libres d'en disposer: il ne s'agit pas de nous uniquement, et nos intérêts sont mêlés d'ordinaire avec les intérêts des autres. Elle a besoin d'une grande justesse pour ne livrer pas nos amis en nous livrant nous-mêmes, et pour ne faire pas de présents de leur bien dans la vue d'augmenter le prix de ce que nous donnons. ("De la confiance," RD 194; see Appendix 125)

Confidence in others is a rare commodity because it involves a loss of autonomy and a willingness to compromise and to alter behavior for the good of all. Difficult as this cooperation may be, it is the only way to create the climate of mutual respect upon which both close friendships and social harmony depend.

In "De la confiance," La Rochefoucauld analyzes the process by which the confidence we gain from the sincerity of others allows us to forge links with our fellow citizens that enable us to live together with them without totally giving up the pursuit of our own interests. Placing confidence in others is an absolute necessity, in both friendship and social life, but it must be subject to strict limitations and maintained with great prudence:

> La confiance plaît toujours à celui qui la reçoit: c'est un tribut que nous payons à son mérite; c'est un dépôt que l'on commet à sa foi; ce sont des gages qui lui donnent un droit sur nous, et une sorte de dépendance où nous nous assujettissons

volontairement. Je ne prétends pas détruire par ce que je dis la confiance, *si nécessaire entre les hommes puisqu'elle est le lien de la société et de l'amitié;* je prétends seulement y mettre des bornes, et la rendre honnête et fidèle. Je veux qu'elle soit toujours vraie et toujours prudente, et qu'elle n'ait ni faiblesse ni intérêt; je sais bien qu'il est malaisé de donner de justes limites à la manière de recevoir toute sorte de confiance de nos amis, et de leur faire part de la nôtre. (RD 195; emphasis mine; see Appendix 126)

By exchanging confidence with others we can go a long way toward overcoming the distrust and bad feelings created by the deceit and trickery so often practiced in society. In a world where artifice and disguise exist almost everywhere, it is only through the generation of such mutual confidence, built up over time from the sincerity displayed by all concerned, that true friendship or a workable form of social organization of any kind can be forged.

Useful Lies

Truth, *Honnêteté,* and the Social Contract

> ... *pero el constante varón juzga por especie de*
> *traición el disimulo; préciase más de la tenacidad*
> *que de la sagacidad: hállase donde la verdad se*
> *halla* ...
>
>   Gracián, *Oráculo manual y arte de prudencia*[†]

One of the central ethical problems La Rochefoucauld addresses
is how to reconcile his view of society as a world of perpetual
illusion-making and mutual deceit with his belief that truthfulness and sincerity are what distinguish the real *honnête homme*
from the ambitious trickster who is wearing only the mask of
honesty and honor. Since life in society is to a large extent a
battlefield on which the conflicting interests and desires of individuals must somehow be accommodated, human beings must
find some way to resolve the tensions and rivalries that always
arise among the members of a given society, each of whom is
motivated much more by self-love and self-interest than by
generosity and altruism. Without that resolution, society will
simply not survive. As many critics have pointed out,[1] La
Rochefoucauld's attempt to formulate a theory of *honnêteté*
comes into conflict with his firmly held belief that human action is determined by self-love and that the world is governed
by self-interest. In trying to set out the duties and responsibilities
of the *honnête homme,* the author of the *Maximes* is clearly on
the horns of a dilemma: the *honnête homme* as he defines
the concept is, above all, a lover and seeker of truth, but La

---

[†] ... the honest man, however, regards dissimulation as a kind of
treason; he sets more store by tenacity than shrewdness; he is to be found
where truth is to be found ... (*The Oracle,* trans. Walton)

Rochefoucauld is forced to admit that in social life it is not always advisable to speak the truth under all circumstances. The nature of society sometimes brings even the most sincere and honest of people to the realization that when social harmony is at stake, lying can often become a useful and productive enterprise.

Because it is so difficult to ascertain the true motives behind the actions of others (and very often behind our own as well), it is virtually impossible to know which actions are really inspired by sincerity or *honnêteté* and which are the result, not of truthfulness and honesty, but of cleverness and cunning:

> Il est difficile de juger si un procédé net, sincère et honnête est un effet de probité ou d'habileté. (M 170; see Appendix 127)

Such difficulties explain in large part why society can be a very frustrating place in which to live, as Alceste in Molière's *Le Misanthrope* (*The Misanthrope*), for example, learns. For the moralist, the inability of most human beings to distinguish between true and false *honnêteté* makes the task of defining what it means to be *honnête* a laborious and complicated one. If it can never be certified that what appears to be an act of sincerity or honesty is in fact motivated by such laudable instincts, it becomes all the more difficult to assess the conditions under which the real *honnête homme* (in the wide meaning given to the term in the seventeenth century) operates and to determine the values that he should espouse.

Apart from a few maxims devoted to the topic, La Rochefoucauld's theories concerning *honnêteté* and its close connections to the concepts of sincerity and confidence are to be found in the *Réflexions diverses*. As Paul Bénichou writes in "L'Intention des *Maximes*," the originality of La Rochefoucauld's contributions to the long debate on the nature of *honnêteté* lies in the fact that he "sent, plus qu'aucun autre, sur quelles ruines" (36) ("senses, more than anyone else, on what ruins") his theory is constructed. It is quite true that much of what La Rochefoucauld has to say about the human condition and the nature of truth seems to preclude his wanting to promulgate a theory of *honnêteté* founded on individuals' love of truth or willingness to expose their true character and feelings to the scrutiny of others. Nevertheless, it is possible to reconcile these two conflicting dimensions of La Rochefoucauld's work. Moreover, the doctrine of *honnêteté* outlined in the *Réflexions* can be seen as stemming "en droit fil des tristes découvertes des *Maximes*" (Rosso, *Procès à La Rochefoucauld* 161) ("directly from the sad discoveries of the *Maximes*"). Part of the solution to the problem lies in the fact that when he discusses the attributes and accomplishments of the *honnête homme,* La Rochefoucauld is describing an ideal world in which many of the weaknesses and failings of humanity are counterbalanced by a passionate desire on the part of the various members of society to live and work together in peace and harmony. Like Thomas Hobbes, he fully understood that trying to realize the ideal of *honnêteté* involves working out a precarious balance between the individual's self-interest and the need to ensure that society will continue to function harmoniously for the benefit of all.

* * *

In La Rochefoucauld's eyes, the concept of *honnêteté* begins with our willingness to resist the long-standing human preference for disguise and deceit, a stance which leads us to project as accurate an image as possible of our faults and weaknesses. This self-revelation is what distinguishes the true *honnête homme* from the countless imposters, the genuine article from the thousands of worthless imitations:

> Les faux honnêtes gens sont ceux qui déguisent leurs défauts aux autres et à eux-mêmes. Les vrais honnêtes gens sont ceux qui les connaissent parfaitement et les confessent. (M 202; see Appendix 128)

It is in attempting to define this sometimes nebulous concept of *honnêteté* that La Rochefoucauld finds himself grappling with some very puzzling and frustrating ethical issues. How does the *honnête homme* resist the forces of self-love? How does he compensate for the essential falsity that is at the heart of the human condition? Must the *honnête homme* be sincere and forthright at all times or are there limits to such exceptional and, for most human beings at least, totally unnatural behavior?

Unlike most of his contemporaries, who tended to emphasize civility, politeness, and honorable behavior as the key elements in the concept of *honnêteté*,[2] La Rochefoucauld places great emphasis on the need to act in a sincere and unpretentious manner, to avoid at all costs pretending to be something one is not:

> Le vrai honnête homme est celui qui ne se pique de rien.
> (M 203; see Appendix 129)

Clearly La Rochefoucauld sees a close and important connection between the concept of *l'être vrai,* the genuine person who reveals to others who he or she really is, and the ideal of the *honnête homme,* who embodies many other traits, but whose essence lies in the twin virtues of sincerity and lack of pretension. Human beings, as La Rochefoucauld describes and defines them, are creatures who are always ready to camouflage their true identity as well as assume an identity to which they have no legitimate claim. This elaborate process of dissimulation, ostentation, and self-aggrandizement may take on various forms but in most cases it continues unabated throughout life. The *honnête homme* or *honnête femme* is that rare person who can successfully overcome such powerful instincts and behave, most of the time at least, in a manner that is neither affected nor ostentatious.

How a person behaves in front of others, La Rochefoucauld believes, reveals much more than the extent of his or her knowledge of the rules of etiquette or the code of courtly deportment; it reveals the underlying character of the person as well. The true *honnête homme* does not shirk his social responsibilities and is willing at all times to expose his character and conduct to the scrutiny of others:

> C'est être véritablement honnête homme que de vouloir être toujours exposé à la vue des honnêtes gens. (M 206; see Appendix 130)

In other words, the *honnête homme* is, above all, a social creature, always eager to take part in the process of social intercourse, to interact with his peers in the interests of society as a whole. This process is what La Rochefoucauld calls *le commerce des honnêtes gens* ("interaction among honest people").

In "De la société," La Rochefoucauld outlines at some length the rules governing *le commerce des honnêtes gens.* Although friendship and social intercourse are different in some respects, they still present similarities, since they both involve interaction and mutual respect among individuals:

> Mon dessein n'est pas de parler de l'amitié en parlant de la société; bien qu'elles aient quelque rapport, elles sont néanmoins très différentes: la première a plus d'élévation et de dignité, et le plus grand mérite de l'autre, c'est de lui ressembler. Je ne parlerai donc présentement que du *commerce particulier que les honnêtes gens doivent avoir ensemble.* (RD 185; emphasis mine; see Appendix 131)

This aspect of La Rochefoucauld's theory of *honnêteté* is not, of course, entirely original. Many of his contemporaries, especially Méré, also suggested how *les honnêtes gens* should interact with each other. La Rochefoucauld, however, takes us well beyond the concept of *honnêteté* as such into his ideas on the proper functioning of society and on the steps that must be taken to preserve social harmony.

As might be expected, La Rochefoucauld acknowledges that some form of *politesse* is required in social situations, particularly in the discussion and debate that take place in a literary *salon.* The main purpose of such polite behavior is to avoid shocking or offending others in the midst of a heated argument:

> Il y a une sorte de politesse qui est nécessaire dans le commerce des honnêtes gens; elle leur fait entendre raillerie, et elle les empêche d'être choqués et de choquer les autres par de certaines façons de parler trop sèches et trop dures, qui échappent souvent sans y penser, quand on soutient son opinion avec chaleur. (RD 187; see Appendix 132)

Ostensibly, such politeness is designed only to keep the art of conversation at as peaceful and civilized a level as possible. However, as we have seen in the previous chapter, the rules that govern the verbal exchange of ideas also apply to other spheres of human activity. For La Rochefoucauld, there is little difference between the methods used to preserve peace and harmony when conversing with others and those required when indulging in other more elaborate or more generalized forms of social intercourse.

When *les honnêtes gens* converse with each other, they must have confidence in each other's willingness to obey the rules of polite conversation. The confidence exchanged at this level is not substantially different from the confidence that, at the level of society as a whole, enables human beings to work together for the common good:

> Le commerce des honnêtes gens ne peut subsister sans une certaine sorte de confiance; elle doit être commune entre eux; il faut que chacun ait un air de sûreté et de discrétion qui ne donne jamais lieu de craindre qu'on puisse rien dire par imprudence. (RD 187; see Appendix 133)

To be *honnête* means both to inspire this kind of confidence in others and to have it oneself. In conversation, as in other forms of social intercourse, the bonds established between people must be based on mutual trust and on at least the expectation of mutual benefit.

What La Rochefoucauld has to say about the various forms of wit that exist in the world also applies not only to the art of conversation but also to other human endeavors that bring people into contact, and therefore potentially into conflict, with others. In both cases, the primary objective is to create and to preserve harmony:

> Il faut de la variété dans l'esprit: ceux qui n'ont que d'une sorte d'esprit ne peuvent plaire longtemps. On peut prendre des routes diverses, n'avoir pas les mêmes vues ni les mêmes talents, pourvu qu'on aide au plaisir de la société, et qu'on observe la même justesse que les différentes voix et les divers instruments doivent observer dans la musique. (RD 187; see Appendix 134)

In a concert, musicians may be playing different instruments, but as long as these are well tuned and played with precision, the overall effect produced will be a pleasurable one. In conversation, as in other aspects of social life, the individual talents and efforts of all concerned contribute to the general good, provided that they are coordinated in a way that promotes the "pleasure" and the interests of all.

* * *

In setting out the principles upon which a stable and productive society is based, La Rochefoucauld describes the steps the members of such a society must take to counteract the divisive and ultimately destructive forces that would be unleashed if the self-interest of each of them were allowed to remain unrestricted and unrestrained. In "De la société," he underscores the importance of seeking to control self-love, one's own and that of others:

> Il serait inutile de dire combien la société est nécessaire aux hommes: tous la désirent et tous la cherchent, mais peu se servent des moyens de la rendre agréable et de la faire durer. Chacun veut trouver son plaisir et ses avantages aux dépens des autres; on se préfère toujours à ceux avec qui on se propose de vivre, et on leur fait presque toujours sentir cette préférence; c'est ce qui trouble et qui détruit la société. Il faudrait du moins savoir cacher ce désir de préférence, puisqu'il est trop naturel en nous pour nous en pouvoir défaire; il faudrait faire son plaisir et celui des autres, ménager leur amour-propre, et ne le blesser jamais. (RD 185; see Appendix 135)

Social life thus becomes a process of accommodation and compromise. Since we all seek our own "pleasure and advantages" at the expense of others, some means must be found to avoid the battles which thinkers such as Hobbes see as the inevitable outcome of unbridled self-interest. It is impossible to eliminate completely the "preference" we feel for our own needs as opposed to those of others, but we can at least mitigate the effects of this preference by concealing it as often and as effectively as possible.

Besides self-interest and all its terrible consequences, many other factors tend to divide the members of a society. Such divisions make working together more difficult and the chances of durable social harmony more remote. La Rochefoucauld chooses to discuss two such factors: differences in mental attitude or mind, in "humor" or personality, and differences in social class or "personal qualities." In any social group, he contends, there will always be different types of mind and people of radically different "humors." Such differences are, of course, potential sources of conflict that must be carefully considered and, if possible, counterbalanced:

> Le rapport qui se rencontre entre les esprits ne maintiendrait pas longtemps la société, si elle n'était réglée et soutenue par le bon sens, par l'humeur, et par des égards qui doivent être entre les personnes qui veulent vivre ensemble. S'il arrive quelquefois que des gens opposés d'humeur et d'esprit paraissent unis, ils tiennent sans doute par des liaisons étrangères, qui ne durent pas longtemps. (RD 186; see Appendix 136)

Similarly, differences in social class or ability should not be overlooked. As much as possible, those who are superior in position or talent should try not to abuse the advantages they have over other people. Such an attitude toward the less privileged and the less talented members of society exhibited by a French aristocrat during the reign of Louis XIV would have represented a rare exception to the view held by most of La Rochefoucauld's contemporaries:

> On peut être aussi en société avec des personnes sur qui nous avons de la supériorité par la naissance ou par des qualités personnelles; mais ceux qui ont cet avantage n'en doivent pas abuser; ils doivent rarement le faire sentir, et n'en servir que pour instruire les autres; ils doivent les faire apercevoir qu'ils ont besoin d'être conduits, et les mener par raison, en s'accommodant autant qu'il est possible à leurs sentiments et à leurs intérêts. (RD 186; see Appendix 137)

Coming from a *duc et pair,* this is a truly extraordinary statement, revealing an attitude toward the lower echelons of society that contrasts sharply with that of the memorialist Saint-Simon, for example, several decades later. Admittedly, while this passage shows considerable sympathy for the less fortunate in society, little doubt remains as to who must continue to exert both influence and political power over whom.

Whatever the relationship between individuals and different social classes may be, La Rochefoucauld maintains that it is absolutely necessary that every person's personal freedom be preserved. Because of all the possible sources of friction between human beings who choose to live in a community, the members must learn to work and play together:

> Pour rendre la société commode, il faut que chacun con- serve sa liberté: il faut se voir, ou ne se voir point, sans sujétion, se divertir ensemble, et même s'ennuyer ensemble; il faut se pouvoir séparer, sans que cette séparation apporte de changement; il faut se pouvoir passer les uns des autres, si on ne veut pas s'exposer à embarrasser quelquefois, et on doit se souvenir qu'on incommode souvent, quand on croit ne pouvoir jamais incommoder. (RD 186; see Appendix 138)

The idea that one should not bother others unduly (a point which La Rochefoucauld also raises in the *Maximes*) seems to suggest that this is a natural characteristic of most human beings and one that must be vigorously counteracted. If it is not, society will soon fall back into what Hobbes describes as a "condition of Warre" (*Leviathan* 202).

It is equally important to be indulgent toward others, whenever the circumstances warrant, but not too indulgent, or else the preservation of individual freedom, upon which the efficient functioning of society directly depends, will be compromised. The rights and needs of others must always be taken into consideration, but only up to a point:

> Il faut contribuer, autant qu'on le peut, au divertissement des personnes avec qui on veut vivre; mais il ne faut pas être toujours chargé du soin d'y contribuer. La complaisance est nécessaire dans la société, mais elle doit avoir des bornes: elle devient une servitude quand elle est excessive; il faut du moins qu'elle paraisse libre, et qu'en suivant le senti- ment de nos amis, ils soient persuadés que c'est le nôtre aussi que nous suivons. (RD 186–87; see Appendix 139)

In discussing the measures that must be taken to ensure the smooth functioning of society and the preservation of social harmony, La Rochefoucauld is prepared to admit the necessity of making the individual's motives appear to be different from what they really are, of sacrificing, temporarily at least, the unquestioning devotion to truth that he sees as the true mark of the *honnête homme.*

* * *

Using terms and formulating his ideas in a manner that strangely foreshadows the great debates on the subject during the coming Enlightenment, La Rochefoucauld suggests that self-love and self-interest, which he describes as normally wreaking havoc on the altruistic impulses of human beings to the point of almost destroying all hope of maintaining social harmony, can nevertheless, under certain circumstances, motivate the individual to contribute to the common good. In the *Maximes* and in "De la société," he does not deny that the self-interest that often pushes us into succumbing to our vices can also often act as the principal motivating factor behind our good deeds:

> L'intérêt que l'on accuse de tous nos crimes mérite souvent d'être loué de nos bonnes actions. (M 305; see Appendix 140)

The common good is produced by the actions of individuals, all of whom seek to further their own interests and accomplish their own very private goals, just as victory in battle is achieved through the combined efforts of individual soldiers, each of whom is primarily interested in finding his own private path to glory:

> Ceux qui voudraient définir la victoire par sa naissance seraient tentés comme les poètes de l'appeler la fille du Ciel, puisqu'on ne trouve point son origine sur la terre. En effet elle est produite par une infinité d'actions qui, au lieu de l'avoir pour but, regardent seulement les intérêts particuliers de ceux qui les font, puisque tous ceux qui composent une armée, allant à leur propre gloire et à leur élévation, procurent un bien si grand et si général. (MS 41; see Appendix 141)

When it comes to explaining how the diverse interests of the members of a given society either come into conflict with each other or somehow complement and reinforce each other's strengths and weaknesses, La Rochefoucauld is forced to recognize both the possible positive effects of actions motivated by self-interest and the possible disadvantages and drawbacks of excessive sincerity and an unlimited, exaggerated, or obsessive devotion to the cause of truth. This is precisely the position taken by Philinte in *Le Misanthrope.*

In order to reduce the friction between individuals produced by their opposing needs, La Rochefoucauld suggests taking a number of measures designed to demonstrate to others our willingness to take their opinions and feelings into account:

> Comme il est malaisé que plusieurs personnes puissent avoir les mêmes intérêts, il est nécessaire au moins, pour la douceur de la société, qu'ils n'en aient pas de contraires. On doit aller au-devant de ce qui peut plaire à ses amis, chercher les moyens de leur être utile, leur épargner des chagrins, leur faire voir qu'on les partage avec eux quand on ne peut les détourner, les effacer insensiblement sans prétendre de les arracher tout d'un coup, et mettre en la place des objets agréables, ou du moins qui les occupent. ("De la société," RD 187; see Appendix 142)

At the same time one should be very careful not to become too closely involved in the affairs of others, not to try to learn more about them than they know themselves. Discussing others' problems with them should be done only within very strict limits:

> On peut leur parler des choses qui les regardent, mais ce n'est qu'autant qu'ils le permettent, et on y doit garder beaucoup de mesure; il y a de la politesse, et quelquefois même de l'humanité, à ne pas entrer trop avant dans les replis de leur cœur; ils ont souvent de la peine à laisser voir tout ce qu'ils en connaissent, et ils en ont encore davantage quand on pénètre ce qu'ils ne connaissent pas. (RD 188; see Appendix 143)

Such reticence with respect to others' feelings and such reluctance to "penetrate" too deeply into their hearts are not characteristics one would normally associate with a moralist like La Rochefoucauld. In "De la société," however, the author of the *Maximes* presents what he sees as a code of behavior necessary to maintain social peace. Therefore, he is understandably much less concerned with what comes naturally to the average human being.

It is in this context that we must try to assess La Roche-foucauld's contention that it is sometimes necessary to lie. The true *honnête homme* always tries to be as sincere as possible, but in society, situations can easily arise in which knowing the whole truth or letting the whole truth be known can be dangerous and disruptive to social peace. Under normal circumstances, social intercourse provides *les honnêtes gens* with innumerable topics that can be discussed with complete sincerity and honesty. There are always, however, truths that people are afraid of knowing and even more afraid of making public:

> Bien que le commerce que les honnêtes gens ont ensemble leur donne de la familiarité, et leur fournisse un nombre infini de sujets de se parler sincèrement, personne presque n'a assez de docilité et de bon sens pour bien recevoir plusieurs avis qui sont nécessaires pour maintenir la société: on veut être averti jusqu'à un certain point, mais on ne veut pas l'être en toutes choses, et *on craint de savoir toutes sortes de vérités.* (RD 188; emphasis mine; see Appendix 144)

Some truths are so painful and so potentially harmful to the mutual confidence, the "Covenant of mutuall trust" (*Leviathan* 202), as Hobbes puts it, on which social harmony depends, that it may be better for all concerned if they are quietly and discreetly suppressed. When an individual is forced to choose between the love of truth and the good of society, it may be better to refuse to disclose the truth and even, in some circumstances, to lie.

Chapter Nine

La Rochefoucauld and Posterity

The Continuing Debate

On doit exiger de moi que je cherche la vérité,
mais non que je la trouve.

Diderot, *Pensées philosophiques*[†]

Jener ist auf der Jagd, angenehme Wahrheiten zu
haschen, dieser—unangenehme. Aber auch der
Erstere hat mehr Vergnügen an der Jagd, als an
der Beute.

Nietzsche, *Morgenröthe*[‡]

Since La Rochefoucauld's death, the issues he raised about the difficulties we all face in trying to discover the truths of everyday life and, in a wider context, the debate about the nature of truth to which he made such an important contribution have continued to fascinate, provoke, and inspire his readers. In the eighteenth century, his *Maximes* continued to be widely read and hotly debated, although they were often misunderstood by an age whose preoccupations and priorities were, in many respects, very different from his. Even though Vauvenargues, for example, derived a great deal of his inspiration directly from La Rochefoucauld, his criticisms of his predecessor's ideas were strongly worded and far-reaching. La Rochefoucauld went too far, Vauvenargues claims, in trying to caution his readers against the falsity of most human virtues:

[†] I am required to search for truth, but not necessarily to find it.

[‡] This one is hunting pleasant truths, that one unpleasant. But even the former takes more pleasure in the hunt than in the booty. (*Daybreak*, trans. Hollingdale)

> Qu'elles qu'aient été ses intentions, l'effet m'en paraît perni-
> cieux; son livre, rempli d'invectives délicates contre l'hypo-
> crisie, détourne, encore aujourd'hui, les hommes de la vertu,
> en leur persuadant qu'il n'y en a point de véritable. (1: 173;
> see Appendix 145)

Even though Vauvenargues and his contemporaries often re-
proached La Rochefoucauld, somewhat unfairly, for having tried
to "séparer notre intérêt personnel de celui de l'humanité" (1:
399–400) ("separate our personal self-interest from the interests of humanity"), they nevertheless enthusiastically carried
on the debate about the relation between private interests and
public good.

Among the many issues upon which La Rochefoucauld had
expressed his views, the problem of truth in moral matters and
the serious difficulties its unmasking can involve continued to
intrigue French moralists throughout the eighteenth century.
While the optimism of moralists like Vauvenargues generally
lead them to believe much more strongly than La Rochefoucauld
in the positive effects of *amour-propre,* others, like Chamfort,
professed at least as deep a cynicism as La Rochefoucauld's
concerning the possibilities of ultimately discovering the truth
in human affairs. Virtue, says Chamfort, can be attained, but
truth is another matter:

> L'homme peut aspirer à la vertu; il ne peut raisonnablement
> prétendre de trouver la vérité. (127; see Appendix 146)

Like La Rochefoucauld, Chamfort sees *homo sapiens* as a creature who naturally and eagerly fosters illusions about himself,
who disguises his true feelings and motives at every opportunity, and yet who manages, sometimes at least, to catch glimpses
of the truth, both about others and about himself:

> Il y a des hommes à qui les illusions sur les choses qui les
> intéressent sont aussi nécessaires que la vie. Quelquefois
> cependant ils ont des aperçus qui feraient croire qu'ils sont
> près de la vérité; mais ils s'en éloignent bien vite, et res-
> semblent aux enfants qui courent après un masque, et qui
> s'enfuient si le masque vient à se retourner. (120; see Ap-
> pendix 147)

Chamfort is closely following La Rochefoucauld's lead whenever he associates the concept of the mask with the process of searching for truth, and he remains as conscious of, and as concerned about, man's ambivalent attitude toward truth as was the author of the *Maximes*.

Most of the judgments brought down on La Rochefoucauld in the Age of Enlightenment exhibit a very strong reluctance to accept his supposed view of *amour-propre* as "un principe toujours vicieux."[1] At the same time, most eighteenth-century readers agreed that his moral writings do contain a number of irrefutable truths. The article "Intérêt," from the *Encyclopédie,* illustrates the rather mixed reception the *Maximes* received in the eighteenth century:

> . . . M. de la Rochefoucault qui s'exprimoit avec précision et avec grâce, a écrit presque dans le même esprit que Pascal et Nicole; il ne reconnoît plus de vertus en nous, parce que l'amour-propre est le principe de nos actions. Quand on n'a aucun *intérêt* de faire les hommes vicieux; quand on n'aime que les ouvrages qui renferment des idées précises, on ne peut lire son livre sans être blessé de l'abus presque continuel qu'il fait des mots *amour-propre, orgueil, intérêt,* etc. Ce livre a eu beaucoup de succès, malgré ce défaut et ses contradictions; *parce que ses maximes sont souvent vraies dans un sens* . . . (Emphasis mine; see Appendix 148)

This passage reflects the widely held view that La Rochefoucauld had attempted to all but destroy the traditional concept of virtue, and, in a way, that is precisely what he had done. Despite all the disagreements which eighteenth-century thinkers had with many of his ideas, La Rochefoucauld's maxims were still seen by most of them as containing a number of significant and highly useful truths.

Although La Rochefoucauld's detractors were no doubt more numerous than his admirers throughout most of the eighteenth century, there was an increasing awareness, on the part of many of his readers, that La Rochefoucauld had achieved an understanding of the human psyche which far surpassed that of his contemporaries. Many people began to realize that even though La Rochefoucauld may have written, in many respects, "in the same spirit as Pascal and Nicole," he had nevertheless made an important series of discoveries about human nature and about the unseen forces motivating human behavior. In a series of detailed commentaries on the *Maximes* published in Amsterdam in 1772, the journalist Jean Manzon expressed his century's ambivalent attitude toward La Rochefoucauld in this way:

> Ce grand homme eut beaucoup de desagrémens à essuyer; on l'accusa d'avoir empoisonné le motif des plus belles actions, et de vouloir corrompre la vertu jusques dans sa source: Mais enfin, la vérité a triomphé de l'ignorance et de l'hypocrisie; et l'on regarde aujourd'hui le Livre de la Rochefoucault, comme le meilleur et le plus estimable qui ait paru dans son genre.[2] (94; see Appendix 149)

Whether or not La Rochefoucauld had set out to "corrupt virtue right to its very source," it cannot be denied that many of his pronouncements on the subject call into question the very existence of virtue in the traditional sense of the word. In the opinion of Manzon, and in that of many of his contemporaries, La Rochefoucauld's originality in this and in other areas of moral philosophy is incontestable:

> Avant lui, on avoit écrit sur le cœur de l'homme, on avoit peint ses passions, ses vices et ses vertus; mais on n'avoit envisagé que les effets, sans remonter jusques à la source. On connoissoit les jeux, tantôt nobles et sublimes, tantôt honteux et bas, ridicules, bizarres, surprenans, quelquefois uniformes en apparence, mais toujours infiniment divers, de cette machine compliquée qu'on appelle le cœur humain; et cependant on ignoroit le ressort unique et simple, qui la fait mouvoir. (94; see Appendix 150)

This "ressort," this "unique" motivating force, is of course self-love, in all its "infinitely diverse" manifestations and incarnations. As Manzon clearly understood, what is new in La Rochefoucauld is the attempt to look beyond the "effects" of our passions, vices, and virtues to their causes, their "source," however difficult it may be to reach them.

Despite his shortcomings, Manzon argues, La Rochefoucauld surpasses all other moralists in getting at the hidden motives of human behavior and, therefore, the *Maximes* must be seen as a work far more valuable than any other currently in print:

> Il y a plus de choses, plus de vérités dans cet ouvrage, que
> dans tous les Livres de Morale ensemble; et il suffiroit, s'il
> étoit bien médité, pour mener à une connoissance parfaite
> de soi-même, de son propre cœur, et de celui des autres. (95;
> see Appendix 151)

For Manzon, a materialist but a sometime admirer of Rousseau,
the *honnête homme* was no longer seen as the embodiment of
all the characteristics of *l'être vrai;* rather he put his faith in
l'homme sensé, the sensible, rational being whom the thinkers
of the Enlightenment believed would eventually solve all human problems. The sensible man is the one who does not allow his "humor" to affect his judgment, who does not allow
what he knows to be the truth to be disguised or distorted in
any way:

> L'homme sensé peut avoir de l'humeur, mais elle ne l'éblouit
> pas jusqu'à lui faire confondre le vrai et le faux: il fait que
> la vérité n'est pas moins telle, quoique son humeur cherche
> à la lui déguiser . . . (342; see Appendix 152)

In making this perceptive comment, Manzon points out an important distinction which La Rochefoucauld implicitly makes
again and again: the problem is not that truth ever loses its
essence, but that our "humor" of the moment can easily prevent us from seeing the truth, even when it is right before our
eyes. A century after the *Maximes* were first published, La
Rochefoucauld's influence was clearly as strong and pervasive
as ever.

* * *

Since the end of the eighteenth century, La Rochefoucauld has
attracted the attention of many kinds of readers: moral philosophers and novelists, authors of aphorisms primarily interested
in his contributions to the genre, and casual readers of extremely
diverse backgrounds and interests, all of whom have found in
the *Maximes* and in the *Réflexions diverses* an inexhaustible
source of interest and inspiration. Three of these avid readers
of La Rochefoucauld, namely, Lautréamont, Nietzsche, and
Lacan, have themselves exerted a tremendous influence on
present-day attitudes toward language and literature as well as

toward the analysis of the inner and even unconscious workings of the human psyche. For all three major thinkers, reading the *Maximes* was to play a crucial role in their own intellectual development and in the genesis of their own ideas about human beings and the psychological forces that determine our various identities and condition our behavior toward others. All three of them quote, or specifically refer to, a number of maxims of La Rochefoucauld in their own writings, and all make explicit use of his ideas as a means of illustrating or formulating their own arguments and theories. What is particularly striking about these three readers reading La Rochefoucauld is that they all show a strong interest in his proposed solutions to the problem of truth and in his thorough analysis of the human predilection for falsehood and role-playing. Taken together, their reactions to La Rochefoucauld help us to understand how closely the French moralist's views prefigure modern attitudes toward language and modern modes of philosophical inquiry.

In the second *fascicule* of his *Poésies,* published a few months before his death in 1870, the first of these three readers, Isidore Ducasse (better known under his pseudonym, the comte de Lautréamont), "re-writes" three of La Rochefoucauld's maxims in addition to a number of well-known passages in Pascal and Vauvenargues.[3] At first glance, his intention seems to be to turn the three maxims on their heads, to "correct" them in order to show how out of date their ideas are and how little they have to say to the modern generation.[4] However, as is often the case with Lautréamont, there is a great deal here that lies under the surface, much of which can be understood only in the wider context of the *Poésies* as a whole. In this remarkable text, which, like La Rochefoucauld's *Réflexions diverses,* has not received the critical attention it deserves, Lautréamont also meditates at length on the nature of the maxim as a literary form, the function of the moralist, the similarities between the moralist and the poet, and the nature of the truth that poetry— and literature in general—must reflect and attempt to describe. All of these meditations clearly show a strong affinity between Lautréamont and La Rochefoucauld and a much greater understanding on Lautréamont's part of what La Rochefoucauld had tried to do in the *Maximes* than the casual reader of the *Poésies* might at first notice.

In the *Poésies,* Lautréamont reveals his keen interest in how language is used in a densely worded and highly concentrated literary form such as the maxim. In addition to re-writing or "correcting" maxims by La Rochefoucauld, Vauvenargues, and others, he formulates a theory of the genre that is undoubtedly in part a reaction against La Rochefoucauld and the classical form, but which nevertheless also shows how closely he had read and studied the models he holds up as examples of how the maxim should *not* be written. One of the problems with the maxim as a literary form, Lautréamont contends, is that it needs to be enhanced by commentary and analysis, not left as if it were the expression of some eternal, immutable truth:

> Une maxime, pour être bien faite, ne demande pas à être corrigée. Elle demande à être développée. (281; see Appendix 153)

As we shall see, Nietzsche was to perform precisely this function—developing the maxim into a much more complex form in which the idea being expressed is approached from various points of view or extended to other contexts. Once this has been accomplished, the maxim becomes a richly hued and multifaceted literary form.

In his *Poésies,* Lautréamont describes the work of the moralist as being very similar to that of the poet: both are attempting to transcribe onto paper the truths about life that they have learned and that they want to transmit to their readers. In the same passage in which he rewrites La Rochefoucauld's *maxime* 78, Lautréamont proclaims that a talented moralist may be more valuable to society than most poets:

> Mettez une plume d'oie dans la main d'un moraliste qui soit écrivain de premier ordre. Il sera supérieur aux poètes. (283; see Appendix 154)

Moralists resemble poets in many ways, according to Lautréamont, largely because they are primarily interested in the same thing: the practical truths of life. What is important is not what form the presentation of these truths takes—whether it be prose or verse, for example—but rather the connections that the poet or the moralist makes among them:

> La poésie doit avoir pour but la vérité pratique. Elle énonce
> les rapports qui existent entre les premiers principes et les
> vérités secondaires de la vie. (277; see Appendix 155)

While their methods may be quite different, the poet and the
moralist are essentially interested in the same thing and their
chief task is exactly the same: communicating the practical
"truths of life" to the reader. The language used to achieve this
end may be highly polished and elaborately structured, but the
truths it encodes and communicates nevertheless remain simple
and straightforward.

Like La Rochefoucauld, Lautréamont sees the search for truth
as a highly important but extremely difficult enterprise, one
not easily or quickly carried out. For reasons very similar to
La Rochefoucauld's, Lautréamont sees human beings as creatures who desperately need to find the truth, but who often do
not know what to do with it when they find it:

> Rien n'est moins étrange que les contrariétés que l'on dé-
> couvre dans l'homme. Il est fait pour connaître la vérité. Il
> la cherche. Quand il tâche de la saisir, il s'éblouit, se confond
> de telle sorte, qu'il ne donne pas sujet à lui en disputer la
> possession. (287; see Appendix 156)

Interestingly, it is in rewriting a famous passage in Pascal
that Lautréamont expresses a viewpoint very similar to La
Rochefoucauld's. Despite the fact that humans are "made to
know the truth," Lautréamont believes, as does La Rochefoucauld, that truth may be the one thing ultimately beyond their
reach:

> Je ne connais pas d'obstacle qui passe les forces de l'esprit
> humain, sauf la vérité. (280; see Appendix 157)

As is often the case, the extent to which his reading of La
Rochefoucauld may have directly influenced Lautréamont's
ideas about the problem of truth cannot be assessed, especially
given the extensive range of other "intertexts" to which the
latter's work makes frequent reference. However, there can be
little doubt that when he was composing the *Poésies,* Lautréamont was thinking about La Rochefoucauld and his *Maximes,*

assimilating some of the ideas expressed in them while at the same time reacting vehemently against others.

* * *

In the early 1870s, another major figure who laid the groundwork for some of the modern views concerning human motivation and the nature of truth, Friedrich Nietzsche, read La Rochefoucauld with great enthusiasm, incorporating some of the French moralist's maxims and ideas into his notebooks and into two of his greatest works, *Menschliches, Allzumenschliches* (*Human, All Too Human*) and *Morgenröthe* (*Daybreak*). The effect of his reading of La Rochefoucauld on Nietzsche's intellectual development, an influence that has recently been extensively documented,[5] was immediate and decisive. What is particularly significant, for us, is the extent to which Nietzsche was interested in La Rochefoucauld's convictions that most human beings attempt to disguise the true motives behind their actions and in the French moralist's belief that in dealing with human nature, discovering and assessing the truth can be frustrating and, in many cases, ultimately impossible. A considerable body of evidence proves that La Rochefoucauld's *Maximes* directly influenced the evolution of Nietzsche's attitudes toward the aphorism at the stylistic level but also with respect to the German philosopher's growing faith in the aphorism as a powerful means of questioning conventional assumptions about human motivation and of unmasking human beings' predilection for telling lies and deceiving others. As in the case of Lautréamont, Nietzsche's reading of La Rochefoucauld seems to have caused him to react strongly to the French moralist's thought and, as a consequence, to rethink and reformulate his own ideas about the nature of truth.[6]

Although Nietzsche strongly disagreed with many of La Rochefoucauld's theoretical presuppositions and aristocratic prejudices, he nevertheless expresses great admiration for the psychological insights which the *Maximes* provide.[7] In *Menschliches, Allzumenschliches,* he directly associates La Rochefoucauld's contributions to the study of human nature with the complex process of eliminating "psychological error" in order to attain a greater knowledge of truth in the area of human motivation. In discussing the possible conflicts between "serving truth" and "furthering the wellbeing of humanity," Nietzsche quotes La Rochefoucauld:

> der psychologische Irrthum und überhaupt die Dumpfheit auf diesem Gebiete hilft der Menschlichkeit vorwärts, während die Erkenntniss der Wahrheit vielleicht durch die anregende Kraft einer Hypothese mehr gewinnt, wie sie La Rochefoucauld der ersten Ausgabe seiner "Sentences et maximes morales" vorangestellt hat: "Ce que le monde nomme vertu n'est d'ordinaire qu'un fantôme formé par nos passions, à qui on donne un nom honnête pour faire impunément ce qu'on veut." La Rochefoucauld und jene anderen französischen Meister der Seelenprüfung . . . gleichen scharf zielenden Schützen, welche immer und immer wieder in's Schwarze treffen,—aber in's Schwarze der menschlichen Natur. (*Werke* 4.2: 57; see Appendix 158)

Like La Rochefoucauld, Nietzsche is keenly interested in the huge discrepancies he perceives between what *appears* to be the motivation behind human action and what is actually the motivating force. While he ultimately goes much further than La Rochefoucauld in probing the nature and the consequences of such discrepancies, his analysis of the complexity of the situation unquestionably owes much to his reading of the *Maximes*.

In the same work, Nietzsche uses the concept of the mask in much the same way as La Rochefoucauld does, that is, as a symbol of the elaborate camouflage and sophisticated ruses human beings frequently employ to hide from the scrutiny of others the true motives behind their actions. For example, Nietzsche describes how "nobility of bearing" can be used as a mask for envy:

> *Grossheit als Maske.* Mit Grossheit des Benehmens erbittert man seine Feinde, mit Neid, den man merken lässt, versöhnt man sie sich beinahe: denn der Neid vergleicht, setzt gleich, er ist eine unfreiwillige und stöhnende Art von Bescheidenheit.—Ob wohl hier und da, des erwähnten Vortheils halber, der Neid als Maske vorgenommen worden ist, von Solchen, welche nicht neidisch waren? Vielleicht; sicherlich aber wird Grossheit des Benehmens oft als Maske des Neides gebraucht, von Ehrgeizigen, welche lieber Nachtheile erleiden und ihre Feinde erbittern wollen, als merken lassen,

dass sie sich innerlich ihnen gleich setzen. (*Werke* 4.3: 164;
see Appendix 159)

The tone and the content of this maxim are both highly reminiscent of La Rochefoucauld. Such a deliberate and straightforward unmasking of the secret and profoundly selfish
motivations underlying the veneer of respectability that characterizes social intercourse is very much in the spirit of the
Maximes.

It is perhaps even more significant that when Nietzsche seeks
to formulate his ideas on the problem of truth as succinctly as
possible, as in the essay "Ueber Wahrheit und Lüge im ausser-
moralischen Sinne" ("On Truth and Lies in a Normal Sense"),
he stresses, just as La Rochefoucauld does, how difficult it is
to reconcile our penchant for deceit and disguise with our thirst
for truth, given our insatiable vanity:

> die Täuschung, das Schmeicheln, Lügen und Trügen, das
> Hinter-dem-Rücken-Reden, das Repräsentiren, das im er-
> borgten Glanze Leben, das Maskirtsein, die verhüllende Con-
> vention, das Bühnenspiel vor Anderen und vor sich selbst,
> kurz das fortwährende Herumflattern um die eine Flamme
> Eitelkeit so sehr die Regel und das Gesetz, dass fast nichts
> unbegreiflicher ist, als wie unter den Menschen ein ehrlicher
> und reiner Trieb zur Wahrheit aufkommen konnte. (*Werke*
> 3.2: 370; see Appendix 160)

In this passage, Nietzsche's emphasis on wearing a mask and
on role-playing shows just how close his view of human nature is to La Rochefoucauld's and clearly illustrates the close
affinities that exist between the two moralists' ideas, particularly concerning the problem of truth. It need hardly be added
that Nietzsche's views on the subject have strongly influenced
modern thinking about both the human condition and the nature of truth.

Like La Rochefoucauld, Nietzsche believes that human beings' "essential falsity," their innate propensity for lying and
deceit, severely limits their ability to discover the truth about
themselves and about others. He is even more skeptical than
the author of the *Maximes* about the existence of unqualified
truths and about man's ability to discover, understand, and ap-
preciate such truths:

> Ueberzeugung ist der Glaube, in irgend einem Puncte der
> Erkenntniss im Besitze der unbedingten Wahrheit zu sein.
> Dieser Glaube setzt also voraus, dass es unbedingte Wahr-
> heiten gebe; ebenfalls, dass jene vollkommenen Methoden
> gefunden seien, um zu ihnen zu gelangen . . . (*Menschliches,
> Allzumenschliches,* in *Werke* 4.2: 368; see Appendix 161)

Because the true nature of human beings and the true motives
of their actions are hidden behind a veil of illusions and disguises of various kinds, discovering them inevitably involves,
in Nietzsche's view just as in La Rochefoucauld's, a calculated
and complex process of unmasking which became the chief
function of the moralist. The ideal vehicle for expressing the
truths uncovered by this process, as La Rochefoucauld had first
discovered, is the maxim or aphorism.

As Brendan Donnellan has suggested, La Rochefoucauld and
Nietzsche can each be considered "as figures symptomatic of
the break-up of an era" (*Nietzsche and the French Moralists*
69). Like Saint-Simon and Proust, whose writings chronicle
the decline of their respective societies under the pressures of
rapid social change, La Rochefoucauld and Nietzsche each lived
and wrote at times when the social structures of Europe were
undergoing unprecedented change. Both moralists attempted
to cope with the complexities of life in an age in which strongly
held convictions were warring with each other, as Nietzsche
himself put it, and even the aristocratic values they both called
into question—admittedly in very different ways and for very
different reasons—were beginning to lose their appeal. In an
era of instability and uncertainty in social, moral, and intellectual matters, Nietzsche found in La Rochefoucauld a kin-
dred spirit who, two hundred years earlier, had been "as serious,
as conscientious, and as impartial in his search for the truth
about men's real motives" (Donnellan, *Nietzsche and the French
Moralists* 16) as Nietzsche considered himself to be. Their common objectives, as well as the immense differences in style and
substance,[8] make reading the works of La Rochefoucauld and of
Nietzsche together not just a useful exercise in intellectual history, but also a means of gaining greater understanding of the
contributions both made to the study of human nature.

In the wider context of European intellectual history from
the seventeenth century to the present day, it is possible to see
Nietzsche's work, particularly *Menschliches, Allzumenschliches,*

as a key link between the author of the *Maximes* and modern psychoanalytic theory, "a stepping-stone," as Ronald Hayman puts it in his biography of Nietzsche, "between La Rochefoucauld and Freud" (197).[9] Like La Rochefoucauld, Nietzsche makes full use of the maxim or aphorism as a vehicle for expressing the "small, humble truths of human behavior which he has discovered"(Faber 213). Many of these truths, which help to explain the multisided nature of the Self and to define the function of egotism in the determination of human behavior, not only lead directly to Freud but also help the modern reader to perceive much more clearly the close connections that exist between La Rochefoucauld's view of human motivation and some of Freud's most important and most controversial theories. In a very real sense, Nietzsche's reaction to his reading of La Rochefoucauld and the startling and disturbing conclusions he reached as a result laid the groundwork for some of the basic tenets of Freud's theory of psychoanalysis.

* * *

No modern thinker was more acutely aware of the path that leads from the author of the *Maximes* to Nietzsche and from Nietzsche to Freud than was our third reader of La Rochefoucauld, Jacques Lacan, who has probably done more to elucidate Freud's theories and their intellectual origins than any other critic. In his *Séminaires,* Lacan refers to La Rochefoucauld several times. Not surprisingly, Lacan expresses great interest in La Rochefoucauld's theory of *amour-propre,* pointing out that what is original in that theory is the idea that self-love, or egotism, is a frequent source of illusion and deceit:

> Ce qui est scandaleux chez La Rochefoucauld, ce n'est pas que l'amour-propre soit pour lui au fondement de tous les comportements humains, c'est qu'il est trompeur, inauthentique. Il y a un hédonisme propre à l'*ego*, et qui est justement ce qui nous leurre, c'est-à-dire nous frustre à la fois de notre plaisir immédiat et des satisfactions que nous pourrions tirer de notre supériorité par rapport à ce plaisir. ("Psychologie et métapsychologie" 18; emphasis in original; see Appendix 162)

In Lacan's view, this concept of *amour-propre* belongs to a tradition that is not philosophical, but rather one that is parallel to the philosophical tradition, namely, the moralist tradition.

In addition to quoting and discussing La Rochefoucauld, Lacan makes repeated reference in his *Séminaires* to moralists from Gracián to Nietzsche. Although this "tradition" is neither, strictly speaking, a philosophical nor a scientific one, Lacan believes that the work of moralists through the centuries has revealed many truths that can and should be of interest to both the philosopher and the psychoanalyst.

In the same seminar in which he talks about the significance, in modern terms, of La Rochefoucauld's concept of *amour-propre,* Lacan discusses the nature of the work moralists perform and the ways in which their methods parallel those of both the philosopher and the psychoanalyst. Moralists, he says, are not

> des gens qui se spécialisent dans la morale, mais qui introduisent une perspective dite de vérité dans l'observation des comportements moraux ou des mœurs. Cette tradition aboutit à la *Généalogie de la morale* de Nietzsche, qui reste tout à fait dans cette perspective, en quelque sorte négative, selon laquelle le comportement humain est comme tel leurré. C'est dans ce creux, dans ce bol, que vient se verser la vérité freudienne. Vous êtes leurrés sans doute, mais la vérité est ailleurs. Et Freud nous dit où elle est. ("Psychologie et métapsychologie" 19; see Appendix 163)

Like the moralist, the philosopher and the psychoanalyst also search for truths disguised as falsehoods. These truths must be unmasked before they can be properly analyzed, categorized, and revealed to others. If both Nietzsche and Freud have been called moralists, it is for good reason. Both, in Lacan's view, performed essentially the same function as La Rochefoucauld: applying "une perspective dite de vérité" to the study of moral behavior and moral codes.

Another of Lacan's seminars deals with the relationship between lies, falsehoods, and errors of all kinds and truth, in a way that is very similar to La Rochefoucauld's *réflexions* on the subject, as well as to Nietzsche's essay "On Truth and Lies in a Normal Sense." Like La Rochefoucauld, Lacan is concerned with the implications of the fact that truths are almost always bound up inextricably with lies and errors,[10] that finding truths inevitably involves unmasking and denouncing the lies and errors which always serve, in one way or another, to disguise them. Paradoxically, without such a process of untangling and unmasking, the truth would be even more difficult to perceive or to define:

> En effet, à mesure que le mensonge s'organise, pousse ses tentacules, il lui faut le contrôle corrélatif de la vérité qu'il rencontre à tous les tournants du chemin et qu'il doit éviter. La tradition moraliste le dit—il faut avoir bonne mémoire quand on a menti. Il faut savoir bougrement de choses pour arriver à soutenir un mensonge . . .
>
> Mais ce n'est pas encore le véritable problème. Le véritable problème est celui de l'erreur, et c'est là, de toujours, qu'il s'est posé.
>
> Il est clair que l'erreur n'est définissable qu'en termes de vérité. Mais il ne s'agit pas de dire qu'il n'y aurait pas d'erreur s'il n'y avait pas de vérité, comme il n'y aurait pas de blanc s'il n'y avait pas de noir. Les choses vont plus loin— il n'y a pas d'erreur qui ne se pose et ne s'enseigne comme vérité. ("La Vérité surgit de la méprise" 289; see Appendix 164)

In the eternal search for truth in human affairs, the methods of investigation and analysis have changed since La Rochefoucauld's time, but the problems that those who search for it must face, whether they be moralists, philosophers, or psychoanalysts, remain essentially the same.

* * *

The reactions of Lautréamont, Nietzsche, and Lacan to La Rochefoucauld's ideas both about the nature of truth and about the countless obstacles that the search for truth can entail clearly reveal the enormous impact La Rochefoucauld has had on modern attitudes toward the problem of human motivation and the function of the moralist in modern society. For these three major figures are not the only intellectual giants of their time to have read La Rochefoucauld with such interest that, like the character Edouard in Gide's *Les Faux-Monnayeurs* (*The Counterfeiters*), they rarely traveled anywhere without a copy of the *Maximes* in their pocket. Many other important thinkers, from Schopenhauer to Barthes, read La Rochefoucauld and, like the three just discussed, discovered in his writings something that is even more apparent to the modern reader than it was to his contemporaries: a fascinating array of insights into the human condition which Barthes has referred to as "un cauchemar de vérité" (*Nouveaux essais critiques* 86) ("a nightmare of truth"). The "nightmare" that La Rochefoucauld describes in his *Maximes* and *Réflexions* is in many ways the nightmare of the Baroque poets, in search of truth in a world of illusion and constant change. It is also the nightmare of modern society.

Chapter Ten

Conclusion

The Modernity of La Rochefoucauld

*L'inquisition et recherche de la vérité est le
propre de l'homme.*
                    La Suite des Marguerites françaises[†]

*Notre cause doit toujours être celle de la vérité,
de quelque façon qu'elle nous soit montrée.*[‡]
                    Mme de Sablé, *Maximes*

Of the many problems La Rochefoucauld addresses in the
Maximes and in the *Réflexions diverses,* the elaborate and infinitely varied disguises that falsehood can wear and the arduous nature of the task of penetrating those disguises in order
to arrive at the truth are both central concepts in his view of
human nature—what we would today call his psychology. As
we have seen in Chapter Eight, these two ideas are also of
vital importance to his views on society, to what might be termed
his "sociology." They should therefore be viewed as the foundation upon which his thought rests, as the ultimate source of
virtually all the fundamental principles that unify his work, even
if they do not necessarily eliminate all the contradictions
embodied in that work. On the one hand, La Rochefoucauld
believes that "nous sommes nais à quester la vérité" (Montaigne
906) ("we are born to quest after truth"), as Montaigne had
shown. On the other hand, experience teaches us that, as La
Bruyère was later to put it, "l'homme est né menteur" (455)
("man is born a liar"). La Rochefoucauld was certainly not the

---

[†] The inquiry and search for truth is the very nature of man.
[‡] Our cause must always be that of truth, no matter how it is revealed
to us.

125

first moralist to be fascinated by the tensions and the drama created by the basic contradiction between humanity's unlimited capacity for falsity and our unquenchable thirst for truth. Indeed, it is a problem that had intrigued Gracián and Montaigne, as well as Descartes and Pascal. What is original about La Rochefoucauld's ideas on the subject is that he manages to show in great detail why it is so difficult to learn the truth about both the thoughts and feelings of others and the real motivation for our own ideas and actions. By suggesting that the Self is heterogeneous and multifaceted and by analyzing in great depth and with a considerable degree of originality the internal and external forces that determine human behavior, he demonstrates clearly and convincingly how the vagaries and the complexities of human nature serve to subvert the individual's search for truth. Most modern readers of La Rochefoucauld, including Lacan, would agree that he succeeds in carrying out the demonstration with a degree of insight and a depth of understanding rarely equaled. At the same time, as we have seen in the last chapter, his views on self-love and on the arbitrary nature of language—particularly as it is used to describe moral conduct—make him a direct precursor of more recent and highly influential thinkers who have felt the need to undertake a similar broadly based inquiry into the nature of truth.

The modernity of La Rochefoucauld lies, among other things, in the extent to which he is able to show in precise terms just how problematic and how frustrating the process of searching for truth can be when the field of inquiry is human nature and human behavior rather than the objective reality that is the domain of the scientist. In sharp contrast to Descartes, La Rochefoucauld is not at all sure it is ever possible to acquire reliable information about the true motives of others let alone about our own. General principles may be drawn from a study of human nature, he believes, but there is no guarantee that those principles will apply in all cases:

> Il est plus aisé de connaître l'homme en général que de connaître un homme en particulier. (M 436; see Appendix 165)

Coming from a moralist, this is a surprising and profoundly disturbing statement. Furthermore, while we may be inclined to believe the flattering things our friends say about us, it may be, La Rochefoucauld claims, that our enemies see much more deeply into our hearts and minds than we will ever be able to do:

> Nos ennemis approchent plus de la vérité dans les jugements qu'ils font de nous que nous n'en approchons nous-mêmes. (M 458; see Appendix 166)

Such pessimism about the possibilities of finding the truth in moral and ethical matters has appalled some readers of La Rochefoucauld and led them to condemn what they consider to be his moral nihilism. Ironically, it is precisely this same pessimism that appeals to many modern readers of his work, for they have come to see in La Rochefoucauld a forerunner of modern attitudes toward writing, language, and the process of understanding the inner and often unconscious workings of the human psyche.

* * *

One of those readers, Roland Barthes, makes the point that whether one reads the maxims of La Rochefoucauld in isolation from each other ("par citation" ["by quotation"], as he puts it) or as a single text, like a narrative or essay, they nevertheless exhibit a fundamental discontinuity, the causes of which run much deeper than the simple fact that the maxim is a discrete unit, "un bloc général composé de blocs particuliers" (Barthes, "La Rochefoucauld" 71) ("a large block composed of smaller ones"). Underlying each of these discrete units is "un discontinu plus subtil" ("a more subtle form of discontinuity") which originates both in the subtleties of La Rochefoucauld's style and in the complexity of the ideas he is trying to express. Because this underlying discontinuity invests the text with an element of instability (what Barthes calls "une mobilité infiniment sensible d'éléments clos" ["Littérature et discontinu" 181] ["an infinitely perceptible mobility of discrete elements"]), it undermines the carefully balanced "architecture" of the maxim form. Although he does not use the term, what Barthes is describing is nothing less than the eruption of Baroque aesthetic principles and practices in the midst of what has traditionally been considered a quintessentially "classical" literary form. As in the case of many Baroque literary works from the poetry of Jean de Sponde to the essays of Montaigne, the multileveled discontinuity of the *Maximes* forces readers to piece together for themselves the various parts of a very complex puzzle.

The discontinuity that characterizes the *Maximes* is directly related to another important dimension of the work, which also has its roots in Baroque discourse: its "openness."[1] To the modern reader, much of the appeal of the *Maximes* stems from the fact that it is in many ways an "open" work, like Molière's *Dom Juan,* a text that functions on many different levels and therefore one that lends itself to a multiplicity of interpretations.[2] In a letter addressed to Edith Mora in which he refers to La Rochefoucauld as "ce grand Ouvert" (Mora 123) ("this great Open One"), René Char emphasizes that the status of the *Maximes* as an "open work" explains why La Rochefoucauld has been read and admired by so many modern writers, beginning with André Gide. More recently, André-Alain Morello has argued that it is largely because of this "openness" that La Rochefoucauld can be seen as a distant but direct precursor of modernism. The ambiguity and the eclecticism of the *Maximes* make it, in other words, a thoroughly "modern" work:

> Œuvre complexe qui échappe à toute interprétation définitive . . . Œuvre polysémique, qui rassemble des discours venus d'horizons différents et qui les transpose dans le code éminemment énigmatique de la maxime. Ce "grand obscur" de notre XVIIᵉ siècle . . . est aussi un grand précurseur de notre modernité. (126; see Appendix 167)

* * *

This enigmatic and open-ended literary form was precisely the instrument La Rochefoucauld needed to express his views on the nature of truth and his profound skepticism concerning all attempts to find and to define the truth. Between the multileveled, discontinuous, and ambiguity-laden form of the *Maximes* and La Rochefoucauld's concept of truth, there exist a number of very close and extremely important links. Just as every human being must uncover the hidden motives and carefully concealed passions and vices of his fellow human beings, the reader of the *Maximes* must attempt to find, under the hidden

layers (or "folds," as Deleuze puts it) of the maxims he is studying, the invaluable truths they contain. Because La Rochefoucauld sees truth as both relative and unstable, his maxims
present his views on the nature of truth in a discontinuous and
dynamic manner that contrasts sharply with the "hard" and
tightly structured form one normally associates with the term
maxim. In a strange but very direct way, the process of uncover-
ing the hidden truths of the *Maximes,* one that all readers experience, directly mirrors the process of unmasking the truth
experienced by all human beings in real life.

If there is a "system" in La Rochefoucauld's thought, it is
one that sets out a number of moral principles, some of which
fit together very well and some of which appear to contradict
each other directly. So it is with the search for truth. Some
universal truths do exist, but since most truths do not exist in
pure form (that is, uncontaminated by falsehoods of one kind
or another), it is difficult if not impossible to find a set of moral
principles that applies in all cases and that does not evolve, at
least to some degree, over time. In La Rochefoucauld, the search
for truth is hampered not just by the nature of truth itself, but
also by the inefficient and unreliable means human beings have
at their disposal for identifying truths and by the often conflicting interests of the various other selves of which the Self
is composed. As Baroque writers from Gracián to Montaigne
had shown, the Self is a complex and constantly changing entity that has all kinds of reasons for not wanting to know the
truth and for seeking to conceal those truths of greatest importance both from itself and from others.

Within the human psyche, powerful forces are constantly at
work to dissuade the individual from satisfying his or her "will
to truth." As La Rochefoucauld untiringly attempts to prove,
self-love is such a powerful force that it can easily overcome
our will to uncover the truth, either by doing its best to make
the truth more difficult to distinguish from falsehood or by simply subverting the processes by which the individual attempts
to unmask the truth. At the same time, the many passions to
which all human beings must succumb, whether they admit it
or not, perform a similar function, by destabilizing our mental
and emotional states and thereby reducing all of us to creatures
driven by desire. Similarly, the infinite variety of ways in which

vices masquerade as virtues undermines our ability to distinguish between the two. The result is that we are even less able to recognize true virtue when we see it than we would otherwise be. In all of these areas, the will to truth is inevitably compromised by some of the elemental forces that make up human nature.

When we enter into relationships with others, our self-love, our changing passions, and our secret vices combine with human "essential falsity," as Francis Jeanson puts it, to create a being who functions very well in society, but who is fundamentally a fraud. The *être vrai* who lurks inside each of us is so heavily disguised and so highly motivated to frustrate every attempt we make to unmask its true identity, that social life becomes a masked ball at which almost no one drops his or her mask. Alone with themselves, humans have countless reasons for disguising the truth from themselves. In society, they have even more reasons for disguising it, both from themselves and from others. Because these "all too human" truths are so painful, the moralist takes on a decidedly dangerous and ultimately thankless task: making others understand more fully their basic inner forces. If this can be accomplished, it will be easier for all concerned to cope with the never-ending task of separating truth from falsehood, of distinguishing between the disguises falsehood always wears and the truths they so effectively conceal. To a greater extent than any of his contemporaries, La Rochefoucauld makes us acutely aware of the formidable obstacles we face whenever we set out to unmask the truth.

Appendix

English Translations

These English translations for the longer quotations are keyed to the text by number.

1 Truth and falsehood are alike in face, similar in bearing, taste, and movement; we look upon them with the same eye.

2 What does this mean if not that the spectacle of man gives him, through an immediate intuition, a feeling of *falsehood*, and that his whole psychology is nothing but the formulation of that intuition?

3 It should be noted that the truth in question is not transcendental, essentially metaphysical, but relative and practical: each individual must maintain his own truth, as it is determined by his temperament, by his social position, by the circumstances in which he finds himself. This is why truth is inseparable from the idea of being natural; it is harmony, whereas falsehood is disproportion.

4 Even when they designate themselves as "philosophers," the moralists of the seventeenth century . . . do not indulge in speculation, in meta-physics. *Like philosophers, they devote themselves to the "search for truth,"* but it is not extension, motion, the characteristics of reason, or occasional causes which interest them. The moralist limits himself to the relative, the contingent, the concrete, the accidental, and above all to *that which has been lived.*

5 TRUTH. That which is essentially true. It is in this sense that one says that God is the truth, the essential truth, the eternal truth.

6 TRUTH, in a more ordinary sense is contrasted with error, false opinion, and signifies, a true and certain proposition; a constant and irrefutable dogma; a clear and obvious maxim; knowledge of the nature of things. It refers to the mysteries of Religion as well as to the knowledge acquired through study, or meditation. The truths of Religion must be implanted early in the mind . . .

MALEB[ranche]. We grope for the truth: we see only the appearances of it . . . LA ROCH[efoucauld]. *The most general classification which has customarily been made of the various philosophical sects is to distinguish among those who believed they had found the truth, those who thought it cannot be found, and those who, thinking they had not found it, nevertheless searched for it all their lives* . . .

7 TRUTH, also refers to sincerity, to good faith in the relating of particular or personal facts; events; incidents; the circumstances of what is happening: *in this case it is contrasted with lies, disguises, deceit.* The accused was able to hide and disguise the truth so well, that he could not be convicted of a crime which no one doubted he had committed . . . NIC[ole]. *We would like to have the glory which comes from loving truth, and the satisfaction produced by never hearing it* . . .

8 in this work, there is a great deal of wit, very little goodness, and *many truths* of which I would have been ignorant all my life, had I not been made to see them.

9 it is a very fertile ground for *an infinite number of beautiful truths* that one has the pleasure of digging up through meditation.

10 If the *Maximes,* moreover, did not contain, if not all the truth, at least so many truths, why have they been attacked so often?

11 Baroque discourse—and this is its dominant characteristic—seeks to convince and to persuade . . . , to bring about an intellectual and/or emotional response. *But this persuasive discourse also presents itself as a discourse of Truth.*

12 Man is therefore nothing but disguise, deceit and hypocrisy both in himself and in his relations with other people. He does not want to be told the truth; he avoids telling it to others . . .

13 In this atmosphere, the *Maximes* of La Rochefoucauld represent a lofty, but secretly powerless, effort to preserve the greatness of man while remaining meticulously and systematically wary of all illusions.

14 while it is agreed that men have, in place of mind, a permanent illusion, the moralist, for his part, is endowed with the ability to transcend this chaos of individual illusions.

15 INCONSTANCY. f. n. A lack of firmness, of durability, of resolution. *Inconstancy* is a defect of the soul which makes it change, sometimes for the worse, sometimes for the better.

16 INCONSTANT, adj. Lacking in firmness, in constancy. Fortune is *inconstant.* Lovers are usually *inconstant.*

17 We come newborn to every milestone of life's journey, and often act like novices at each, no matter what our age.

18 We are sometimes *inconstant* through a fickleness and weakness of mind which allows us to accept the opinions of others; and sometimes, which is more excusable, through a growing distaste for the world.

19 The *revolving* years change men's intellectual tastes no less than their worldly fortunes.

20 No one sees with the same eyes that which touches him and that which does not; our taste is led along by the inclination of our self-love and our humour, which provide us with new views, and enslave us to *an infinite number of changes and uncertainties*; our taste is no longer ours, we no longer possess it, it changes our will, and the same objects appear to us from so many angles with which we are unfamiliar that we end up not knowing what we have seen and what we have felt. (CF)

21 Bodily traits follow a determined course *which affects and imperceptibly modifies our will. They run in harness* and exercise a secret domination over us, so that without our knowing it they play a great role in all our actions.

22 We perceive only *the fits of emotion and extraordinary movements of our humours,* such as violence, anger, etc. . . .

23 It seems that Fortune, *however changeable and capricious it is*, renounces these changes and caprices in order to act in concert with Nature, and that the two of them come together from time to time to produce extraordinary and exceptional men, to serve as models for posterity. (CF)

24 Does the death of M. de Turenne, so appropriate to such a distinguished life, accompanied by so many singular circumstances and occurring at such a critical point in time, not seem to us to be the result of the fear and *uncertainty of Fortune*, which did not dare to decide the fate of France and of the Empire? (CF)

25 but when this mask is torn off, and he refers things to truth and reason, he [the individual] will feel his judgment as if it were all upset, and nevertheless restored to a much surer status.

26 MASK. A piece of black velvet with openings for the nose and eyes, used by Ladies to cover their face when they go out in the country or the town.
———. This word has other fine figurative meanings.
———. His respectability is only a *mask* used to deceive with more finesse.

27 It seems that it is dangerous to want to declare war against masks. If one takes up the cause of *truth* against them, it is hard to resist the temptation to cast oneself in the most favorable light, which is sometimes too favorable and which may be seen as a mask by a vigilant enemy. It often happens that the defender of truth lets himself be taken over by a kind of excess, in which truth is no longer given its due.

28 One can be false in different ways. There are false men who always want to appear what they are not. There are others, who are more sincere, who were born false, and who never see things as they are. There are some whose intellectual abilities are sound, but whose taste is false. Others are intellectually false, and have somewhat sound taste. And there are others who have nothing false, either in their taste or in their qualities of mind. These last are very rare, since, generally speaking, there is almost no one who does not have a degree of falsity in some area of his mind or of his taste. (CF)

29 What makes this falsity so universal is that our qualities are uncertain and confused, and that our perceptions are as well; we do not see things precisely as they are, we value them more or less than their worth, and we fail to relate them to ourselves in a manner which suits them, and which is appropriate to our situation and to our qualities. This misjudgment places an infinite number of falsehoods into our taste and our minds: our self-love is flattered by everything which presents itself to us in the guise of good; but since there are several kinds of good which affect our vanity or our temperament, we often follow them out of habit or convenience; we seek them out because others are seeking them out, without considering the fact that the same feeling should not be equally embraced by all people, and that we should take it up more or less forcefully, depending on whether it is more or less appropriate to those who are pursuing it. (CF)

30 It is absolutely necessary that there be a voice which is heard, some true or false maxim with which our mind is imbued and which is the guiding principle of our life. It is the nature and the essence of all intelligent beings, to be guided by a light which they recognize; and that is what I call voice. *Their happiness is to be guided by the voice of truth. Their ruin is to let themselves be led by the voice of falsehood.* Thus the duty of all men is to be continually attentive to the voice of truth, in order to follow it; and their dissoluteness consists in listening to and in following the voice of falsehood.

31 We would be wrong to believe that La Rochefoucauld's only intention is to denigrate man; on the contrary, in a state of extreme tension, he aspires to freedom by eliminating through a rigorous self-examination all forms of illusion: an ideal so difficult to attain that the world of true greatness is no longer perceived except by its absence, a closed world whose inhabitants, jealously selected, are afraid to let it be degraded by those who are unworthy of it, and first of all by the possibility that their lucidity may fail.

32 When La Rochefoucauld said of someone that he was genuine [true], he not only meant by that the concept of sincerity, for which the word *sincère* had sufficed, but he also wanted to express the idea that the behavior of an individual must exist in harmony with his true character.

33 Truth, in whatever context it is found, cannot be effaced by comparison with other truths, and whatever difference there may be between the two contexts, what is true in one does not efface what is true in the other: they may be more or less extensive and more or less manifest, but they are always equal by virtue of their being true, which is no more the case in the larger of the two contexts than in the smaller. (CF)

34 A subject can contain several truths, and another subject can contain only one: the subject containing several truths is of greater value, and can shine in places where the other cannot; but to the extent that they are both true, their lustre is of equal brilliance. (CF)

35 Truth is the body and breath of perfection and beauty. Nothing, whatever its nature, can be beautiful or perfect that is not all it ought to be or has not all it ought to have.

36 The maxim is the unmasking of the individual and the revelation of his true character. It usually has two levels and opposes a level of appearances with a level of truth . . .

37 A good maxim is too hard for the teeth of time and whole millennia cannot consume it, even though it serves to nourish every age: it is thus the great paradox of literature, the imperishable in the midst of change, the food that is always in season, like salt— though, unlike salt, it never loses its savour. (*Human* 2: 168)

38 Self-love is the love of self and of everything for the self's sake: it makes men worship themselves and tyrannize, whenever the means are to hand, over others. It finds no rest outside itself and only pauses among outside things as do bees among flowers, to feed upon them.

39 Living everywhere, off anything, off nothing, it is part of every aspect and circumstance of life; it adjusts to what it finds or what it fails to. It even joins the enemy army, enters into their plans and—amazingly—hates itself as they do, plots and helps perpetrate its own destruction. It wants, in brief, only to exist and so long as it does is content to be its own enemy. No wonder then that it often acquires and, to its own ruin, wears in public a self-mortifying look, for in the act of destroying itself in one place it restores itself in another. When it seems to have foresworn pleasure it has only deferred or redirected it, and even when beaten and apparently quite undone, it arises triumphant from its own defeat.

40 The desire to live or to die are appetites of self-love which can no more be contested than the appetites of the tongue, or the choice of colours.

41 Few people are cruel out of cruelty, but all men are cruel and inhuman out of self-love.

42 Self-interest is the soul of self-love, and just as the body, when deprived of its soul, is without sight, without hearing, without consciousness, without feeling and without movement, so does self-love, separated, as it were, from its self-interest, no longer hear nor feel nor move; it is for this reason that a man who travels over land and across the seas in pursuit of his own interests suddenly becomes paralyzed when it is the interests of others which are at stake; it is from this source that come the weariness and the death which we cause in all those to whom we are relating our own affairs; it is from this same cause that results their prompt

resurrection when in our narration we touch on something which concerns them; so that we see in our conversations and in our intercourse with others a man lose consciousness and recover in a single moment, according to whether his own self-interest is or is not affected. (CF)

43 Pride exists equally in all men; the only difference lies in what ways they manifest it.

44 Pride, weary of its poses and its varied shifts, having assumed every role in the human comedy, appears at last without mask and reveals itself through haughtiness. Haughtiness, so to speak, is the bugle and banner of pride.

45 Dissimulation is intensified when its trick has been detected and then endeavours to deceive by means of truth itself: it alters its play by some new feint, and turns simplicity into guile, basing its astuteness upon extreme candour. (*The Oracle* 59)

46 There is no plumbing the depths or piercing the darkness of its abysses; darting in and out of them it escapes the sharpest eye and is often invisible even to itself. All unknowingly it breeds, nourishes, rears a variety of affections and hatreds, some of them so monstrous that when it has brought them to light it fails to recognize or refuses to acknowledge them.

47 Very strange are some of the night-begotten notions it has of itself, while these in turn breed error, ignorance, coarse feelings and silly thoughts on the subject. The next step is for self-love to think its feelings dead when they are merely dormant; to think it would run no longer as soon as it stops to rest; to think it has lost its taste when it has satisfied its craving. But the heavy veil that hides it from itself never prevents its seeing clearly what lies outside; in this it resembles our eyesight, which can see everything but our eyes.

48 As if it were not enough that self-love has the ability to transform itself, it also has the ability to transform its objects; which it does in a surprising way, for not only does it *disguise* them so well that it is itself deceived, but also, as if its actions were miracles, it suddenly changes the nature of things . . .

49 I am convinced that in many situations, it is not without benefit that one looks at what one is doing as theater, and imagines oneself as a character in a play.

50 I see them [the *Maximes*] as the lessons of a master who understands perfectly the art of knowing men, who *sorts out admirably well all the roles they play in society,* and who not only puts us on our guard against the different characters of the theater, but as well who makes us see, by raising a corner of the curtain, that the comedy's lover and the king are the same actors who play the doctor and the buffoon in the farce.

51 Self-interest speaks all sorts of languages and plays all sorts of roles, even that of disinterestedness.

52 Nothing is so impetuous as its desires, so deep-dyed as its schemes, so guileful as its maneuvers; its twisting and turning is beyond words, its altered looks surpass the chameleon's, its subtle blendings outdo the chemist's.

53 Its inclinations alter as do the moods that shape it, that incite it now toward glory, again toward wealth, yet again toward pleasure. Its inclinations alter with age, station, experience of life; but it cares not a whit whether they are single or many since, at need or at will, it can attend to all or concentrate on one.

54 There you have the portrait of self-love, whose whole life is an unflagging turmoil. The sea may be fairly compared to it, in the tireless ebb and flow of whose waves self-love finds an accurate image of its own seething thoughts and its eternal restlessness.

55 We fail to distinguish among various kinds of anger, although there is a mild and almost innocent form, which comes from the ardour of one's complexion, and another truly criminal form, which is, strictly speaking, the fury of pride and of self-love.

56 Whatever fine words we may apply to our afflictions, they all too often derive from selfishness and vanity.

57 Our sufferings are accompanied by various kinds of hypocrisy. In one, under pretext of weeping for the loss of someone we hold dear, we weep for ourselves; we mourn his good opinion of us, the diminution of our possessions, our enjoyments, our prestige. The dead, accordingly, get the credit for tears that really flow for the living. I call this a form of hypocrisy because in such cases *we deceive ourselves.*

58 Our first impulse of joy over the good fortune of our friends springs from neither kindliness in us nor affection toward them, but from

a selfish hope of our being made happy in turn or of our benefit-
ing from our friends' good fortune.

59 Loyalty is a rare invention of self-love, by which man, setting
himself up as a depository for valuable things, makes himself
infinitely valuable. *Of all the dealings of self-love,* it is the one
in which he makes the fewest advances and the largest profits; it
is a refining of his policy, for it commits men by their possessions, by their honour, by their freedom and by their life, which
they are forced to entrust to others on certain occasions, to raising the loyal man above everyone else.

60 Magnanimity is the noble attempt of pride to make man so much
his own master that he can master everything else.

61 There is less love in jealousy than there is self-love.

62 What keeps lovers and mistresses from tiring of being together
is that they talk of nothing but themselves.

63 It is curious that this idea seemed so scandalous, for what was
he saying? He was emphasizing that even what appear to be our
most disinterested activities are performed out of a need for glory,
even love or the most secret exercise of virtue.

64 The most dangerous thing about pride is its way of blinding us;
the more pride swells, the more we lose sight of the remedies for
solacing our misfortunes or for curbing our faults.

65 A proof that men are more aware of their defects than one might
suppose is the fact that they never make a mistake when discussing their own conduct: that same self-love which normally acts
as blinkers now imparts a perfect clarity to their vision, so that
they can suppress or disguise the slightest detail which may cause
them discredit in the eyes of others. (CF)

66 The length of our passions no more rests with us than the length
of our lives.

67 Love is most fitly compared to a fever; with neither can we determine the intensity or the duration.

68 A truly wretched man is he who devotes all his energies to the
gratification of his passions, and so must groan ceaselessly beneath
their yoke. He cannot endure their fury, nor yet the violence he

must do to himself in order to throw off their tyranny. Disgusted by his vices, he is also nauseated by the remedies against them. He can endure neither the pains of sickness nor the rigours of cure. (CF)

69 We far from realize all that our passions make us do.

70 We must notice this carefully, so that, whenever we feel moved by some passion, we suspend our judgment, until it subsides; and that we not let ourselves be easily deceived by the false appearance of the things of this world.

71 When a man has a corrupt heart, all the truths he knows become the instruments of his passions: and far from being useful to him in order to do good, they help color the evil which he does, and to facilitate the execution of his evil designs.

72 Our passions are but the varying fancies of self-love. (CF)

73 With no passion do we show so much selfishness as with love; we are always more willing to sacrifice the other person's peace of mind than to disturb our own.

74 All men's foibles produce only a single vice, which is vanity; and, as the passions of those who move in high society are subordinated to this weakness, this is apparently the reason why there is so little truth in their gestures, in their manners, and in their pleasures. Vanity is what is most natural in all men, and what most often makes them depart from their true nature.

75 We deceive ourselves thinking that only violent passions, like ambition and love, can overpower our other instincts. Indolence, thoroughly languid though it may be, very seldom fails to be master; it interferes with all our plans and actions, and gradually wears down and destroys our passions and virtues.

76 it is the most vicious and intense, however unnoticed its intensity or concealed its ill effects. If we really ponder its power, we see how at every turn it dominates our thoughts, our concerns, our pleasures: it is the sucking-fish that can stop dead great vessels in their progress; it is a lull more dangerous to great enterprises than reefs or violent storms. The passivity of indolence is a secret spell that suddenly disrupts the most enthusiastic pursuits and most stubborn resolves. Indeed, to give a true sense of this force for harm, one must describe it as an inner transport,

the soul's consolation for every hurt and substitute for every blessing.

77 It seems that it is the devil who very deliberately placed indolence on the border between several virtues.

78 I have the greatest respect for fine passions, which are the mark of great souls; and although the disquiet they engender is in some ways antagonistic to strict wisdom, they are so easily linked to the most austere virtues that I do not believe they can be justly condemned.

79 it is mainly the passions which make the best workers excel. When one wants something badly, one looks for the most reliable means of getting it. And it is by this great effort that one makes oneself clever in everything one undertakes.

80 Nature would seem to have hidden deep within us talents and abilities we know nothing about; only strong emotion is able to bring them to light, and to give us at times insights beyond the reach of ordered thought.

81 The passions are no more than varying temperatures of the blood.

82 The indifference we feel toward truth in moral matters results from our being committed to following our passions, no matter what; and this is why we do not hesitate when we must act, despite the uncertainty of our opinions. It matters little, men say, that we know where the truth lies, as long as we know where to find pleasure.

83 We can say of all our virtues what an Italian poet has said of virtue in women, that it is seldom more than the art of appearing virtuous.

84 As we live our lives, vices await us like so many inn-keepers in whose houses we must lodge; and I doubt whether experience would enable us to escape them were we permitted to make the journey twice.

85 What often prevents our being enslaved by a single vice is that we have a number of others.

86 Fortune brings out virtues and vices as light does objects.

87 When our vices desert us, we flatter ourselves that we are deserting our vices.

88 There is a lot of difference between true virtues and those that are only superficial; and there is a lot of difference between the true ones, which result from an exact knowledge of the truth, and those that are accompanied by ignorance or error. The virtues that I call superficial are really, strictly speaking, only vices, which, not being as common as other vices that are their opposites, are usually much more respected than the virtues that are lesser in degree, of which these opposite vices are the extreme.

89 Vices help make up virtues as poisons do medicines. Discreetly tinctured and blended, they become a means of combatting life's ills.

90 it seems to me that the first is this: *that the Réflexions* [the *Maximes*] *destroy all virtues.* One can counter that the intention of their author seems far from wanting to destroy them; he simply claims that he wants to demonstrate that there are almost no pure ones in the world, and that in most of our actions there is *a mixture of error and truth, of perfection and imperfection, of vice and virtue* . . .

91 If vanity does not quite topple the virtues, it leaves every last one of them swaying.

92 Virtues are swallowed up by self-interest as rivers are lost in the sea.

93 We are so preoccupied with our own interests that what we often take for virtues are really only vices which resemble them, *and which our pride and our self-love have disguised.*

94 The invocation of virtue is as useful a weapon in the armoury of self-interest as is vice. (CF)

95 We only condemn vice and praise virtue from a selfish motive.

96 What is commonly called virtue is oftenest a phantom fabricated by our passions and then—that we may do what we want with impunity—given a respectable name.

97 that the virtue of the ancient pagan philosophers . . . was founded on false principles, and that man, so convinced of his own merit, possesses only *the deceptive appearance of virtue* with which he impresses others and by which he is often deceived himself . . .

98 We get so much in the habit of wearing a disguise before others that we finally appear disguised before ourselves.

99 Just as we must keep our distance[s] in order to see the objects around us, we must also keep them with respect to society: each person has his own point of view, from which he wants to be seen; we are right, usually, not to want to be illuminated from up close, and *there is almost no one who, in all matters, wants to be seen as he is.* (CF)

100 We are like shop windows in which we are continually arranging, concealing or illuminating the supposed qualities others ascribe to us—in order to deceive ourselves. (*Daybreak* 172)

101 The world, not knowing what real merit is, shows little interest in rewarding it; thus it elevates to its higher orders and dignities only those who appear to have fine qualities, and it generally gives its highest recognition to that which glitters, even though all that glitters is not gold.

102 People admire that which dazzles, and the art of knowing how to implement mediocre qualities is a means of stealing the esteem of others and of acquiring a greater reputation than real merit would receive.

103 The world more often rewards the appearance of merit than merit itself.

104 To establish oneself in the world, one does all one can to seem established there already.

105 What makes most small children appealing is that they are still wrapped up in the manner and the modes of behaviour which Nature gave them, and that they know no others. They change and corrupt them as soon as they emerge from childhood: they think they must imitate what they see others doing, and they can't imitate it perfectly; there is always something *false* and uncertain in this imitation. They have nothing permanent in their behaviour or in their feelings; instead of actually being what they want to seem, they seek to seem what they are not. (CF)

106 Everyone wants to be someone else, and no longer be what he is: they search for a countenance outside themselves, and a form of wit other than their own; they take on tones and forms of behaviour at random; they experiment with them on themselves, without

thinking that what is appropriate for some is not appropriate for others, that there is no general rule for tones and behaviour, and that there are no good copies. (CF)

107 Two men can nevertheless be similar in several respects without being a copy of each other, if each one follows his natural inclinations; but almost no one follows them completely. We like to imitate; we imitate often, even without realizing it, and we neglect our own talents while going after those of others, which usually do not suit us. (CF)

108 What proves that people know their faults better than we might suppose is that they never confess them in speaking of their conduct: the very vanity which blinds them to self-knowledge, in such moments floods their mind with light, and gives them such thorough insight that they omit or disguise the smallest defect.

109 Men, it would seem, do not think they have faults enough: they add to them by decking themselves out with various peculiarities so carefully cultivated that in the end they become ingrained faults that can no longer be corrected.

110 We should often be ashamed of our noblest actions, if the world but knew all the motives that helped shape them.

111 Moderation comes about through fear of arousing the envy and scorn those people deserve who get drunk on good fortune; it is an empty display of strength of character; further, temperateness in men at the height of their careers is a desire to seem greater than their luck. (CF)

112 Humility is often just a feigned submissiveness employed to dominate others. It is a stratagem of pride, which lowers itself that it may raise itself; and though pride wears a thousand masks, it is never better disguised than when it wears the mask of humility itself.

113 Humility is the true test of Christian virtue: without it we persist in all our faults, concealing them, under a cloak of pride, not only from others but often from ourselves.

114 In most men gratitude is only a secret longing for greater benefits.

115 Love of justice, in most men, is only a fear of encountering injustice.

116 Justice is but a lively fear of losing what belongs to us: hence our consideration and respect for our neighbour's rights and our great care not to cause him damage. Because of such fear, men stay within the bounds set for them by birth and fortune, where otherwise they would continually prey upon others.

117 The clemency of princes is often a mere tactic for gaining their subjects' affection.

118 Kings treat men like so many coins: they give them any value they care to, and one must accept them at the current rate rather than at their actual worth.

119 We are better off exhibiting ourselves as we are than trying to seem what we are not.

120 Sincerity comes directly from the heart. One finds it in very few people; what one usually finds is but a deft pretense designed to gain the confidence of others.

121 Although sincerity and confidence are related, they are nevertheless different in several respects: sincerity is an openness of the heart, which shows us as we are; *it is a love of truth*, a repugnance to disguise oneself, a desire to compensate oneself for one's faults, and even to diminish them by a willingness to admit having them. (CF)

122 One must hide nothing from them regarding that which only concerns ourselves, always appear *genuine* to them with respect to our good qualities and even our faults, without exaggerating the former or diminishing the latter, make it a rule never to make half-confidences; they always embarrass those who make them, and almost never satisfy those who receive them: one gives them confused signals about what one is trying to hide, one sparks their curiosity, one gives them the right to want to know more, and they feel freer to use the secrets they have discovered. It is safer and more honest not to say anything to them than to fall silent when one has begun to speak. (CF)

123 There is a look which suits the appearance and the talents of each person; we always lose something when we drop it to take up another one. We must try to know the one which is natural to us, never abandon it, and perfect it as much as it is possible to do. (CF)

124 What men call friendship is just an arrangement for mutual gain and an exchange of favors: in short, a business where self-interest always sets out to obtain something.

125 Confidence in others leaves us less freedom, its rules are more strict, it requires more prudence and restraint, and we are not always free to possess it: it is not just ourselves who are concerned, and our interests are usually mixed up with those of others. It requires a sound judgment in order for us not to give up our friends' interests when we are sacrificing our own, and for us not to compromise their well-being in the hope of increasing the value of what we are giving up. (CF)

126 Confidence in others always pleases the person who receives it: it is a tribute we make to his merit; it is a deposit we make on our good faith; it is a form of security which gives him certain rights with respect to us, and a kind of dependence to which we submit voluntarily. By saying this, I am not trying to destroy confidence, which is *so necessary between men because it is the bond which creates society and friendships;* I am trying to set limits for it, and make it a matter of honesty and fidelity. I want it to always be genuine and prudent, and to display neither weakness nor self-interestedness; I know that it is difficult to set appropriate limits to the way in which we receive the confidence of our friends, and give them ours.

127 When a man's behaviour is straightforward, sincere and honest it is hard to be sure whether this is due to rectitude or cleverness. (CF)

128 Men who but pretend to be honest hide their faults from others and themselves alike; men who are really honest thoroughly recognize their faults and confess them.

129 A true gentleman is without pretension. (CF)

130 The sure sign of an honest gentleman is the wish that his life be at all times lived in openness with others of his sort. (CF)

131 My intention is not to speak about friendship in speaking about society; although they are somewhat related, they are nevertheless very different: the former has more loftiness and dignity, and the great merit of the latter is to resemble it. I will therefore now speak only about the *particular form of intercourse which honest gentlemen should have with each other.* (CF)

146

132 There is a kind of politeness which is necessary in the intercourse which takes place among honest people; it makes them understand mocking, and it prevents them from being shocked and from shocking others by certain forms of speech which are too abrupt or too harsh, which escape one's mouth without thinking, when one is heatedly defending an opinion. (CF)

133 The interaction among honest people cannot subsist without a certain kind of confidence; it must be shared by all of them; each individual must have an air of reliability and discretion which never gives rise to the fear that he will say something imprudently. (CF)

134 Variety is needed in wit: those who only display one kind of wit cannot continue to please for long. One can take different routes, have different talents, provided that one is contributing to the pleasure of society, and that one is showing the same accuracy that the different voices and the different instruments must show in music. (CF)

135 It would be useless to state how necessary society is to all men: all desire and seek it, but few make use of the means of making it pleasurable and of ensuring that it last. Each person wants to find his own pleasure and advantages at the expense of others; one always prefers himself to those with whom he proposes to live, and one almost always makes them feel that preference; this is what disturbs and what destroys society. One should at least know how to hide this preference, since it is too ingrained in us for us to be able to get rid of it; one must seek his pleasure and that of others, moderate their self-love, and never wound it. (CF)

136 The relationship which is formed between minds would not maintain society for long, if it were not regulated and supported by common sense, by good humour, and by the consideration which must exist between people who want to live together. If it sometimes happens that people of opposing humour or mind seem united, they are no doubt linked by extraneous connections, which do not last long. (CF)

137 One can also find oneself in the company of people to whom we are superior by birth or by personal qualities; but those who have this advantage should not abuse it; they must rarely let it be felt, and only use it to educate others; they must make them see that they need to be led, and lead them by reason, while adapting themselves as much as possible to their feelings and interests. (CF)

138 In order to make society comfortable, it is necessary that each person conserve his freedom: the members of the society must see each other, or not see each other, without constraint, enjoy themselves together, and even be bored together; they must be able to part from each other, without the separation causing any change in their relationship; they must be able to do without each other, if one does not want to expose oneself to occasional embarrassment, and one should remember that one often bothers people, when one thinks he can never bother them. (CF)

139 We must always contribute as much as we can to the entertainment and well-being of the people with whom we want to live; but we must not always be charged with the responsibility of contributing to it. Indulgence is necessary in society, but it must have limits: it becomes a form of servitude when it is excessive; it must at least appear to be freely given, and when we follow the opinion of our friends, they must be persuaded that it is ours that we are following as well. (CF)

140 Selfishness, which we blame for all our crimes, often deserves to be praised for our good deeds.

141 Those who would give victory a family background might be tempted to call it, poetically, the daughter of Heaven, since there is no finding its origin on earth. Certainly it derives from an infinitude of actions which, rather than seeking victory out, look only to the individual interests of the victorious. An army achieves a great victory as a whole through having each man in it seek glory and advancement on his own.

142 As it is difficult for several people to have the same interests, it is at least necessary, for the smooth operation of society, that they not have opposing ones. One must anticipate what will please one's friends, look for means of being useful to them, spare them distress, show them that one shares their distress with them if it cannot be avoided, eliminate it without claiming to remove it at one blow, and put in its place more pleasant concerns, or at least ones which will occupy their time. (CF)

143 One can talk to people about things which concern them, but only to the extent that they permit it, and one must be very moderate in doing so; there is a politeness, and sometimes even a humanity, in not going too deeply into the folds of their heart; they often find difficulty in letting what they know about their own feel-

148

ings be seen, and they have even greater difficulty when one learns what they do not know themselves. (CF)

144 Although the intercourse which honest people have with one another gives them a certain familiarity, and provides them with an infinite number of reasons to speak to each other sincerely, almost no one has the docility and the common sense to receive information about many things which are necessary in order to maintain society: *one wants to be informed up to a certain point, but one is afraid of knowing all kinds of truths.* (CF)

145 Whatever his intentions were, the effect seems to me to be a pernicious one; his book, full of delicate invectives against hypocrisy, still today diverts men from virtue, by persuading them that it does not really exist.

146 Man can aspire to virtue; he cannot reasonably claim to find the truth.

147 There are men to whom illusions about the things which interest them are as necessary as life itself. Sometimes they catch glimpses which would make one think that they are close to the truth; but they quickly distance themselves from it, and resemble children who run after a masked person, and then flee if the person turns around.

148 ... M. de La Rochefoucauld who expressed himself with precision and grace, wrote much in the same spirit as Pascal and Nicole; he recognizes no virtues in us, because self-love is the principle behind our actions. When one has no *interest* in making men vicious; when one likes only works that contain precise ideas, one cannot read his book without being offended by his almost continual abuse of the words *self-love, pride, self-interest,* etc. This book has had much success, despite this defect and its contradictions; *because its maxims are often true in a sense* ...

149 This great man had many annoyances to bear; he was accused of having poisoned the motive behind the greatest actions, and of wanting to corrupt virtue right to its very source: But finally, truth triumphed over ignorance and hypocrisy; and La Rochefoucauld's book is regarded today as the best and soundest of its kind ever published.

150 Before him, people had written about the human heart, they had portrayed its passions, its vices and its virtues; but they had only examined the effects, without going back to the source. People

knew the workings, sometimes noble and sublime, sometimes shameful and low, ridiculous, bizarre, surprising, sometimes uniform in appearance but always infinitely diverse, of this complicated machine which we call the human heart; and yet no one knew the unique and simple motivating force behind it.

151 There are more ideas, more truths in this work, than in all the moral treatises combined; and, well established, it would suffice to lead one to a perfect state of knowledge of oneself, of one's heart, and of the hearts of others.

152 The sensible man can have a certain humor, but it does not dazzle him to the point of causing him to confuse truth and falsehood: he acts in such a way that truth is no less truth, even though his humor seeks to disguise it from him . . .

153 To be well wrought, a maxim does not need to be corrected. It needs to be developed.

154 Put a goose quill in the hands of a moralist who is a first-class writer. He will be superior to poets.

155 Poetry must have for its object practical truth. It expresses the relation between the first principles and the secondary truths of life.

156 Nothing is less surprising than the contradictions in man. He is made to know the truth. He seeks it. When he tries to grasp it, he is so dazzled and confused that no one would envy him the possession of it.

157 I know of nothing which is beyond the reach of the human mind, except truth.

158 psychological error and insensibility in this domain in general promotes humanity, while knowledge of truth perhaps gains for us one more hypothesis such as Larochefoucauld placed before the first edition of his *Sentences et maximes morales:* "Ce que le monde nomme vertu n'est d'ordinaire qu'un fantôme formé par nos passions à qui on donne un nom honnête pour faire impunément ce qu'on veut." Larochefoucauld and the other French masters of psychical examination . . . are like skilful marksmen who again and again hit the bullseye—but it is the bullseye of human nature. (*Human* 1.36)

159 *Nobility as mask.*—With nobility of bearing we provoke our enemies, with unconcealed envy we almost reconcile them with us:

for envy compares, equates, it is an involuntary and groaning kind of modesty.—Has, on account of this advantage, envy ever been assumed as a mask by those who were in fact not envious? Perhaps; it is certain, however, that nobility of bearing is often employed as a mask for envy by ambitious people who would rather suffer disadvantages and provoke their enemies than let it be seen that inwardly they equate themselves with them. (*Human* 2.383)

160 Deception, flattering, lying, deluding, talking behind the back, putting up a false front, living in a borrowed splendor, *wearing a mask,* hiding behind convention, playing a role for others and for oneself—in short, a continuous fluttering around the solitary flame of *vanity*—is so much the rule and the law among men that there is almost nothing which is less comprehensible than how an honest and pure drive for *truth* could have arisen among them. ("On Truth" 80; emphasis mine)

161 Conviction is the belief that on some particular point of knowledge one is in possession of the unqualified truth. This belief thus presupposes that unqualified truths exist; likewise that perfect methods of attaining to them have been discovered . . . ("On Truth" 199)

162 What is scandalous in La Rochefoucauld is not that self-love is for him the foundation of all human behavior, it is that it is deceitful, inauthentic. There is a hedonism peculiar to the *ego,* and which is precisely what deludes us, that is to say deprives us both of our immediate pleasure and of the satisfactions which we could derive from our superiority with respect to this pleasure.

163 people who specialize in morals, but who introduce a perspective "of truth" into the observation of moral behavior and customs. This tradition leads to Nietzsche's *Genealogy of Morals,* which is very much in this rather negative perspective, according to which human behavior as such is deceptive. It is into this hollow, into this bowl, that Freudian truth is poured. You are no doubt deceived, but the truth is elsewhere. And Freud tells us where it is.

164 In fact, as lies are elaborated and push out their tentacles, they must be monitored by the correlative of truth, encountered at every turning and which they must avoid. The moralist tradition says so—one must have a good memory when one has lied. One must know a damned bunch of things in order to successfully maintain a lie . . .

But this is still not the real problem. The real problem is one of error, and it is there, from the beginning, that the problem has arisen.

It is clear that error is definable only in terms of truth. But it is not a question of saying that there would be no error if there were no truth, in the same way that there would be no white if there were no black. Things go much further—there is no error which is not presented and taught as truth.

165 It is easier to know mankind in general than any particular man.

166 Our enemies' opinion of us comes closer to the truth than our own.

167 A complex work which escapes any definitive interpretation . . . A polysemic work, which brings together modes of discourse from different horizons and which transposes them into the eminently enigmatic code of the maxim. This "great unknown" of our seventeenth century . . . is also a great precursor of our modernity.

Notes

Chapter One
Introduction: Truth and Falsehood in La Rochefoucauld

1. Friedrich Nietzsche, *Menschliches, Allzumenschliches,* in *Werke* 4.2: 371; English translation: *Human, All Too Human: A Book for Free Spirits,* trans. R. J. Hollingdale 1: 634. Citation for this and all subsequent references to Nietzsche's *Werke* is by volume, part, and page.

2. All references to La Rochefoucauld are to *Maximes suivies des Réflexions diverses,* ed. Jacques Truchet, unless otherwise specified. Maxims will be cited by source and number. Of the various versions of the text of the *Maximes,* the two to which I will be referring most often are the Liancourt manuscript and the "definitive" edition of 1678, both included in the Truchet edition. Undoubtedly the most important "avant-texte" of the *Maximes,* the Liancourt manuscript provides a number of useful insights into the genesis of La Rochefoucauld's ideas. Selections from this manuscript are designated Liancourt and cited by number. Maxims from the 1678 edition are designated M. The so-called *maximes supprimées* and *maximes posthumes* (designated, respectively, MS and MP and also included by Truchet), are also particularly important sources for this study. Passages from the *Réflexions diverses* will be cited by title, the designation RD, and page number. This edition also contains a number of related texts by other authors (letters, etc.), labeled Truchet ed. and cited by page number.

3. On Augustinian elements in La Rochefoucauld's work, see Jean Lafond, *La Rochefoucauld: Augustinisme et littérature,* and Philippe Sellier, "La Rochefoucauld, Pascal, Saint-Augustin."

4. See Louis Van Delft, "La Rochefoucauld, moraliste mondain" and "Pour une lecture mondaine de La Rochefoucauld."

5. One must not forget that in the *avis au lecteur* (preface) that accompanied the text of the *Maximes* from the second edition on, it is claimed that the author of the *Maximes* has only considered human beings "dans cet état déplorable de la nature corrompue par le péché" (Truchet ed. 5) ("in this deplorable state of nature corrupted by sin"), a disclaimer that supposedly exempts those who are to be touched by divine grace from the very negative image of humanity that the *Maximes* present. Whether this *avis au lecteur,* like most others, should be taken at face value or not is, of course, open to question.

6. "Voilà notre état véritable. C'est ce qui nous rend incapables de savoir certainement et d'ignorer absolument" (*Pensée* 230, Pascal 130) ("This is our true state. It is what makes us unable to know with certainty and to be completely ignorant").

7. The information regarding word frequency in the *Maximes* used in this study was obtained from a computer-assisted lexical analysis of the 1678 edition.

8. According to Vivien Thweatt, ". . . *Du vrai* is more than the opening chapter of the *Réflexions*. It is in many ways the unifying theme of La Rochefoucauld's work" (141).

9. In his book *La Rochefoucauld: The Art of Abstraction,* Philip Lewis talks briefly about "the inextricable intermingling of truth and falsehood" (39) that La Rochefoucauld sees as one of the main problems confronting human beings, both individually and collectively.

10. "Si La Rochefoucauld déplore en l'homme *une essentielle fausseté,* c'est qu'il a choisi d'être un homme supérieur sans avoir à le devenir: comme il redoute de n'apparaître point assez grand, il ne lui reste plus qu'à contester toute apparence, en conservant pour lui le privilège de la vérité" (Jeanson 87) ("If La Rochefoucauld deplores an essential falsity in man, it is because he has chosen to be a superior being without having to become one: since he worries about not seeming great enough, it remains for him to contest every appearance, while keeping for himself the privilege of truth").

11. Letter from Mme de Sablé to La Rochefoucauld, dated 18 February 1665, in La Rochefoucauld, Truchet ed. 582. This passage is quoted by Sainte-Beuve 2: 1259.

12. Some two hundred years later, in notes he was preparing for an essay to be entitled "Der Philosoph" ("The Philosopher"), Friedrich Nietzsche also expresses concern about the far-ranging consequences of what he calls the "Unwahrheit des Menschen gegen sich selbst und gegen andere" (*Werke* 3.4: 77) ("man's falsity toward himself and toward others") (*Philosophy and Truth,* trans. Breazeale 49).

13. Truchet, in the introduction to his edition of the *Maximes* lxvi.

14. Louis Kronenberger, in the introduction to his translation *The Maxims of La Rochefoucauld* 19. Kronenberger's work is the source of the translations of the La Rochefoucauld *maximes* except where the designation CF appears, which indicates I have used the translation by Constantine FitzGibbon, *The Maxims of the Duc de La Rochefoucauld.* FitzGibbon is also the source of the translations of the *réflexions*. All other translations are mine unless a source is given.

15. This *maxime supprimée* (Truchet ed. 133–36) is really much more like a réflexion than a maxim (indeed, it is longer than most of the *Réflexions diverses*). It will be analyzed at some length in Chapter Four.

Chapter Two
La Rochefoucauld and the Baroque Worldview

1. See, for example, Claude-Gilbert Dubois, *Le Baroque: Profondeurs de l'apparence.*

2. Deleuze, *Le Pli: Leibniz et le baroque.* On the concept of the Baroque worldview, see Ch. 3 ("Qu'est-ce qui est baroque?"), 38–54. Deleuze argues convincingly that, like La Rochefoucauld, Leibniz derived many of his most basic ideas and concepts from the Baroque.

3. Thweatt is one of many recent critics who refer to "the Baroque aspects of La Rochefoucauld's thought and style" (216).

4. On the Baroque aspects of La Rochefoucauld's style, see Mary Francine Zeller, *New Aspects of Style in the "Maximes" of La Rochefoucauld* 47–49 and 164.

5. As Truchet suggests in his edition of the *Maximes*, La Rochefoucauld's comparisons between love and either spirits or the Doge of Venice or between vices and hosts in whose home one spends the night could be explained by "a survival of Baroque tastes" (lii).

6. In his edition of the *Maximes,* Rosso questions whether it is possible to call La Rochefoucauld's style Baroque, or to interpret his work in Baroque terms:

> Son effort vers la lucidité, même s'il rencontre beaucoup d'obstacles (qui ne sont jamais minimisés) nous paraît trop évident. Et comment pourrait-on qualifier de "baroque" son langage si essentiel, articulé en des maximes acérées qui vont droit au cœur? (33n103)

> (His effort toward lucidity, even if it encounters obstacles [which are never minimized], seems too obvious. And how could one qualify as Baroque his language, which is so basic and articulated in such biting maxims that go straight to the heart?)

7. "On pourrait rétorquer que La Rochefoucauld est un auteur éminemment anti-baroque. *C'est un fait qu'il entretient des liens très étroits avec la civilisation baroque*" (Rosso, *Procès à La Rochefoucauld* 103; emphasis mine) ("One could counter that La Rochefoucauld is an eminently anti-Baroque author. *It is a fact that he maintains close links with Baroque civilization*").

8. On the Baroque aspects of the *Réflexions diverses,* see Michelle Leconte, "Recherches sur les dates de composition des *Réflexions diverses* de La Rochefoucauld."

9. On the importance of this idea in Baroque literature, see Jean Rousset, *La Littérature de l'âge baroque en France.*

10. According to Felix Freudmann, La Rochefoucauld's formula "is beautifully simple: reality is change, hence belief in constants—moral ones included—is unwarranted. Thus lies at the foot of his system that *ceaseless motion-and-change,* the 'génération perpétuelle' of which Poulet and Bénichou recognized the fundamental importance" (34; emphasis mine).

11. On the concept of taste(s) in La Rochefoucauld, see Michael Moriarty, "La Rochefoucauld: Tastes and their Vicissitudes." La Rochefoucauld's ideas on the subject come close to contradicting each other. If, Moriarty argues, taste is "capricious and irrational, and if it is, as it appears to be, part of the human make-up as such, then how can it also designate a faculty of judgment or discernment?" (120).

12. According to Susan Read Baker, La Rochefoucauld sees in the theory of the *humeurs* "une des causes majeures de l'inconstance de l'homme" (*Collaboration et originalité chez La Rochefoucauld* 85) ("one of the major causes of human inconstancy"). On the links between the theory of the humors and the Baroque concept of *inconstance,* see Lafond, "La Rochefoucauld, d'une culture à l'autre" 156.

Chapter Three
Truth and Its Masks: In Search of *l'Etre Vrai*

1. On mask as metaphor from Spanish Baroque literature to French classicism, see Cioranescu, *Le Masque et le visage: Du baroque espagnol au classicisme français.*

2. On the symbolic meaning of the act of tearing off a mask in Montaigne, see Starobinski, *Montaigne en mouvement* 87–88.

3. The French translation, which was widely read in La Rochefoucauld's time, is entitled: *La Sonde de la conscience, par Daniel Dyke . . . traduit de l'anglois par Jean Vernueil* (Genève: P. Chouet, 1634).

4. "Pour accéder ou espérer d'accéder aux valeurs vraies, il faut impérativement reconnaître en soi toutes les illusions qui nous en détournent" (Lafond, "Dit et non-dit dans les *Maximes*" 206) ("In order to attain or to hope to attain authentic values, one must not fail to recognize in oneself all the ilusions that turn us away from them").

5. On La Rochefoucauld's aesthetic theories, see Mesnard, "L'Esthétique de La Rochefoucauld."

Chapter Four
Self-love, Self-interest, Self-deception

1. On the concept of *amour-propre* in the work of other seventeenth-century French moralists, see Lafond, "L'Amour-propre de La Rochefoucauld (MS 1): Histoire d'un thème et d'une forme." Lafond emphasizes that it is not just in La Rochefoucauld that one finds the idea that "l'amour-propre, dans sa subtilité démoniaque, s'ingère partout, et à tout moment" (267) ("self-love, in its demonical subtlety, infiltrates everywhere and at all times").

2. This is particularly true of the manner in which La Rochefoucauld presents self-love as the primary motivating factor in human behavior and any altruistic tendencies an individual might display as a form of mask designed to deceive others (and, in some cases, oneself). "In a far-reaching Augustinian *critique* of the noble ethic, La Rochefoucauld, as Nietzsche perceived, had made this dichotomy the essential structure of human behavior: egotism, self-interest, self-love, pride, and vanity comprise the essence of a power-seeking humanity, altruism only the mask" (Stanton 68).

3. "In seventeenth-century Europe, the *amor sui* was no longer held to be a pernicious affection of man's soul, but rather the natural trait of the human Self. A radical revolution in the definition of man and his role in the world had occurred and its impact was reflected in all contemporary genres of literature . . ." (Schabert 69).

4. On the affinities between the *Maximes* and the world of the theater, see Weber, "The *Maximes* as Theater," and Morel, "Les *Maximes* et le théâtre" 476.

5. It is ironic, Todorov contends, that the theater, which Pascal considered to be one of the virtuous person's greatest enemies, becomes, in La Rochefoucauld, the very means by which the moralist comes to understand the life of the individual and the functioning of society (47).

6. In his definition of the term *trafic,* Pierre Richelet specifies that it refers primarily to the buying and selling of various kinds of privileges, a practice rampant in seventeenth-century France and which, according to Richelet, is nothing less than "shameful" (*honteux*).

7. A thought-provoking analysis of Lacan's reading of La Rochefoucauld is provided by Serge Doubrovsky in "Vingt propositions sur l'amour-propre: De Lacan à La Rochefoucauld."

Chapter Five
A Theory of the Passions

1. Richelet defines *passion* as "a general term that refers to agitation produced in the soul by the movement of the blood" ("mot general qui veut dire agitation qui est causée dans l'âme par le mouvement du sang . . ."). Furetière explains that in moral matters the word *passion* describes "the different movements of the soul according to the objects that present themselves to one's senses" ("[les] differentes agitations de l'âme selon les divers objets qui se presentent à ses sens"). The lexicographer also distinguishes two major categories of passions: the "concupiscible appetites" (sensual pleasure, pain, greed, love, and hate) and the "irascible appetites" (anger, fear, hope, despair).

2. Nietzsche, *Morgenröthe* 5.479, in *Werke* 1: 288 (*Daybreak: Thoughts on the Prejudices of Morality,* trans. Hollingdale 197).

3. On the many close connections between Vauvenargues and La Rochefoucauld, see Peter Martin Fine, *Vauvenargues and La Rochefoucauld.*

4. On this point, see Martin 116.

5. "PARESSE. Est aussi un vice moral, une nonchalance, une faineantise, une delicatesse qui empêche de faire son devoir, ou de vaquer à ses affaires . . ." (Furetière) ("INDOLENCE. Is also a moral vice, a nonchalance, a laziness, a delicacy which prevents one from doing one's duty, or attending to one's affairs . . ."). In his dictionary, Pierre Richelet quotes this maxim, illustrating thereby the extent to which La Rochefoucauld was being read at the time.

6. "La paresse est une prison subtile où l'homme ne reconnaît même pas quelquefois son manque de liberté . . ." (Toner, "La Question de l'utilité dans les *Maximes* de La Rochefoucauld" 22) ("Indolence is a subtle prison in which man sometimes doesn't even recognize his lack of freedom . . .").

7. In *De la recherche de la vérité (In Search of Truth,* 1674), Nicolas Malebranche suggests that truth and falsehood are always closely bound up with each other and that under the "inspiration" of passion, truth quickly dissipates but falsehood is somehow preserved:

> Dans les jugements qui précèdent les passions, le vrai et le faux sont joints ensemble; mais lorsque l'âme est agitée, et qu'elle juge selon toute l'inspiration de la passion, le vrai se dissipe et le faux se conserve, pour servir de principe à d'autant plus de fausses conclusions que la passion est grande. (2: 144)

> (In the judgments we make before we experience passion, truth and falsehood are joined together; but when the soul is agitated and judges everything according to the inspiration of passion, truth disappears and falsehood is preserved, in order to serve as a guiding principle to as many false conclusions as the passion is strong.)

Chapter Six
Vices and Virtues

1. On the nature of this association, see Susan Read Baker, "La Rochefoucauld et Jacques Esprit."

2. "Il y a des vertus intellectuelles, morales, heroiques, Cardinales, Téologales. Les vertus Cardinales s'apellent de ce nom, parce qu'elles sont les principales et la source des autres. Les vertus cardinales sont la prudence, la justice, la temperance et la force . . ." (Richelet) ("There are intellectual, moral, heroic, cardinal, and theological virtues. The cardinal virtues are so called because they are the principal ones and the source of the others. The cardinal virtues are prudence, justice, temperance, and strength . . .").

3. Richelet defines *vice* as "habitude contraire à la vertu. Défaut qui est oposé à la vertu" ("a habit contrary to virtue, a fault that is opposed to virtue").

4. "A la Sérénissime Princesse Elisabeth," dedication to *Principes de la philosophie* (Descartes 87–88).

5. Corrado Rosso emphasizes La Rochefoucauld's use of the word *frontières* to describe the overlapping and interweaving that takes place between virtues and vices, the result of "una fondamentale contiguità fra vizi e virtu" (*Virtu e critica della virtu* 27) ("a fundamental contiguity between vices and virtues").

6. In the outline for an essay entitled "Der letzte Philosoph" ("The Last Philosopher"), Nietzsche makes the following statement, undoubtedly inspired by his reading of La Rochefoucauld: "Die Welt der Lüge—

die Wahrheit kommt allmählich zum Rechte—*alle Tugenden entstehen aus Lastern*" (*Werke* 3.4: 85; emphasis mine) ("The world of lies—truth gradually comes into its own—*all virtues grow out of vices*" [Plan for "The Last Philosopher," Winter 1872–Spring 1873, in *Philosophy and Truth* 155]).

7. La Rochefoucauld, Letter to le père Thomas Esprit, 6 February 1664 (Truchet ed. 578).

8. As Tilo Schabert points out, La Rochefoucauld asks throughout the *Maximes* "how it can be that his contemporaries all behave according to the rules of the courtly mode of life *and yet are anything but paragons of virtue*" (72; emphasis mine).

9. "It is in La Rochefoucauld's treatment of these social virtues," Henry C. Clark maintains, "that he launches what amounts to a coherent attack on the teleological pretensions of his aristocracy" (69).

Chapter Seven
Disguising the Truth from Others

1. In Pierre Nicole's *Essais de morale,* which were strongly influenced by La Rochefoucauld, as well as by the Fathers of the Church, it is suggested that those who move about in high society are particularly prone to using ruses of all kinds in order to get what they want:

> Les gens du monde, qui sont animés d'un autre esprit, ont coutume au contraire de *cacher leurs véritables sentimens,* comme dit Saint Gregoire, et d'user d'une infinité de détours et de finesses pour arriver où ils prétendent. (3: 26; emphasis mine)

> (On the contrary, people in high society, who are of another frame of mind, are accustomed to *hiding their true feelings,* as Saint Gregory said, and using an infinite number of subterfuges and subtleties to reach their goals.)

2. This is another point to which Vauvenargues returns in his *Réflexions et maximes:*

> Nous sommes trop inattentifs, ou trop occupés de nous-mêmes, pour nous approfondir les uns les autres: quiconque a vu des masques, dans un bal, danser amicalement ensemble, et se tenir par la main sans se connaître, pour se quitter le moment d'après, et ne plus se voir ni se regretter, peut se faire une idée du monde. (2: 437)

> (We are too inattentive, or too occupied with ourselves, to really come to know each other: whoever has seen masked dancers, at a ball, dancing together amicably, and holding hands without knowing each other, then taking leave of each other a moment later, never to see or miss each other again, can have some idea of what society is like.)

3. In *De Cive* (1651), Thomas Hobbes contends that it is men's "mutuall fear" and "mutuall will of hurting" which necessitates their entering into a contract or covenant with the other members of society in order to preserve social harmony (45–53).

4. La Rochefoucauld's emphasis on the concept of openness seems to have had considerable influence on the definition of the term *sincérité*. Pierre Richelet quotes *maxime* 62 in its entirety in his definition of the word, and Furetière also includes the idea of openness in his definition of the adjective *sincère:*

> SINCERE. Qui est franc, qui parle à cœur ouvert, sans feinte ni dissimulation. Je vous ay donné un advis sincere. On se peut fier à luy, c'est un homme sincere.

> (SINCERE. Refers to he who is frank, who speaks with an open heart, without feigning or dissimulation. I gave you some sincere advice. He can be trusted, he is a sincere man.)

5. La Rochefoucauld is of course not the only moralist of his time to promote the cause of sincerity and frankness in all things. Like La Rochefoucauld, the chevalier de Méré sees sincerity as an essential trait of the *honnête homme:*

> Je ne trouve rien de si beau, que d'avoir le cœur droit et sincère. Il me semble que c'est le fondement de la sagesse . . . et prenez garde que de certaines gens, qui ont tant de plis et de replis dans le cœur, n'ont jamais l'esprit juste: il y a toujours quelque faux jour qui leur donne de fausses veues. Et puis l'artifice et les ruses témoignent qu'on n'a pas assez de talent pour faire ce qu'on veut par les belles voies. Le parti qui plaist aux honnestes gens est celuy de la franchise et de la simplicité. (1: 52)

> (I find nothing so beautiful as to have a sound and sincere heart. It seems to me to be the foundation of wisdom . . . and take care that some people, who have many folds in their hearts, never have a sound mind: there is always some light that gives them a false view of reality. And then artifice and ruses demonstrate that one doesn't have enough talent to do what one wants in the right way. The stance that appeals to "honnestes gens" is that of frankness and simplicity.)

Chapter Eight
Useful Lies: Truth, *Honnêteté,*
and the Social Contract

1. Serge Doubrovsky alludes, for example, to the contradictions and complications arising from "le désir de La Rochefoucauld de promouvoir une morale de l''honnêteté,' après avoir assigné tout l'humain aux fureurs

de l'amour-propre" (211) ("La Rochefoucauld's desire to promote an ethical code based on 'honnêteté,' after having relegated all that is human to the powerful forces of self-love").

2. Richelet defines the term as follows: "Civilité, manière d'agir polie, civile et pleine d'honneur, procédé honnête et qui marque de la bonté" ("Civility, a polite, civil and honorable mode of behavior, conduct which shows honesty and goodness").

Chapter Nine
La Rochefoucauld and Posterity:
The Continuing Debate

1. "Intérêt," *Encyclopédie ou dictionnaire raisonné des sciences, des arts et des métiers.*

2. Although Manzon was a minor figure, a hack writer rather than a serious critic, his analyses of the *Maximes* are perceptive and intelligent.

3. The three "re-written" maxims are:

[1] C'est une preuve d'amitié de ne pas s'apercevoir de l'augmentation de celle de nos amis. (Lautréamont 280)

(It is a proof of friendship not to notice that our friends' feelings of friendship toward us have increased.)

[La Rochefoucauld, MS 66]

[2] Si nous n'avions point de défauts, nous ne prendrions pas tant de plaisir à nous corriger, à louer dans les autres ce qui nous manque. (Lautréamont 280)

(If we had no faults, we would not take such pleasure in correcting them, in praising in others that which is lacking in us.)

[La Rochefoucauld, M 31]

[3] L'amour de la justice n'est, en la plupart des hommes, que le courage de souffrir l'injustice. (Lautréamont 283)

(The love of justice, in most men, is only the courage to suffer injustice.)

[La Rochefoucauld, M 78]

4. As Gérard Genette suggests in *Palimpsestes,* this rewriting is in fact a form of parody. Genette uses the term *parodie réfutative* (Genette 47–52).

5. See Brendan Donnellan, *Nietzsche and the French Moralists,* and Marion Faber, "The Metamorphosis of the French Aphorism: La Rochefoucauld and Nietzsche."

6. The similarities and affinities between Lautréamont and Nietzsche go far beyond their reading of the *Maximes.* According to Ronald Hayman, Nietzsche's early fragment "Euphorion" "strikingly prefigures Lautréamont's *Les Chants de Maldoror* (1868)" (47).

7. Nietzsche is not the only major figure in nineteenth-century German intellectual history to express interest in La Rochefoucauld: Corrado Rosso ("Une Rencontre devant les rayons d'une bibliothèque: La Rochefoucauld et Marx") quotes a letter from Marx to Engels in which Marx refers to eight maxims of La Rochefoucauld.

8. See Brendan Donnellan, "Nietzsche and La Rochefoucauld."

9. On the general contexts of this fascinating connection, see Anne-Marie Desfougères, "Des moralistes à la psychanalyse."

10. This explains, among other things, his great interest in the writings of Gracián.

Chapter Ten
Conclusion: The Modernity of La Rochefoucauld

1. In an essay devoted to "Tacite et le baroque funèbre," Barthes describes as Baroque "un système ouvert, soumis à la fois à une structure et à un procès" ("an open system, subject both to a structure and to a process"), a system that both proliferates "de tous côtés" ("on all sides") and is subject to some overriding unifying force. This is precisely what is going on in the *Maximes* (*Essais critiques* 111).

2. In a recent article, Lafond stresses the importance of this aspect of the *Maximes:*

> La maxime heureuse, la maxime réussie n'impose pas arbitrairement un sens, elle ouvre un champ, à la limite inépuisable comme les interprétations auxquelles peut se prêter le texte. D'autant que l'architecture du livre, de par sa discontinuité, n'impose pas un parcours linéaire: le lecteur est sollicité, appelé à la construction d'un sens, mais cette construction n'est jamais achevée . . . ("Mentalité et discours de maîtrise, ou le moraliste en question" 323)

> (The good maxim, the successful maxim does not arbitrarily impose a meaning, it opens up a field of possible meanings, a virtually inexhaustible one, like the interpretations to which the text lends itself. Just as the architecture does not, because of its discontinuity, impose a linear route: the reader is asked or called upon to construct a meaning, but this process of construction is never finished . . .)

Select Bibliography

Works by La Rochefoucauld

Editions

La Rochefoucauld, François de. *Maximes.* Ed. Corrado Rosso. Firenze: Sansoni, 1968.

———. *Maximes et autres œuvres morales.* Pref. Jacques de Lacretelle. Paris: Bordas, 1949.

———. *Maximes et mémoires.* Introd. Jean Starobinski. 10/18. Paris: Union générale d'éditions, 1964.

———. *Maximes suivies des Réflexions diverses.* Ed. Jacques Truchet. Paris: Garnier, 1967.

———. *Œuvres complètes.* Introd. Robert Kanters. Ed. L. Martin-Chauffier. Bibliothèque de la Pléiade. Paris: Gallimard, 1964.

———. *Œuvres de La Rochefoucauld.* Ed. D. L. Gilbert, J. Gourdault, A. Régnier, and H. Régnier. Collection des Grands Ecrivains de la France. Paris: Hachette, 1868–83. 4 vols.

———. *Réflexions ou sentences et maximes morales. Réflexions diverses.* Ed. Dominique Secretan. Textes littéraires français. Genève: Droz, 1967.

———. *Réflexions ou sentences et maximes morales, suivi de Réflexions diverses et des Maximes de Mme de Sablé.* Ed. Jean Lafond. Folio. Paris: Gallimard, 1976.

Translations

La Rochefoucauld, François de. *The Maxims of La Rochefoucauld.* Trans. and introd. Louis Kronenberger. New York: Random, 1959.

———. *The Maxims of the Duc de La Rochefoucauld.* Trans. Constantine FitzGibbon. London: Millington, 1974.

———. *Moral Maxims and Reflections, in Four Parts.* Written in French by the Duke of Rochefoucault. Now made English. London: M. Gillyflower, 1694.

Critical Studies and Other Works

Bacon, Sir Francis. "Of Truth." *The Essayes or Counsels, Civill and Morall.* Ed. and introd. Michael Kiernan. Oxford: Clarendon, 1985. 7–9.

Baker, Susan Read. *Collaboration et originalité chez La Rochefoucauld.* Gainesville: U of Florida P, 1980.

Baker, Susan Read. "La Rochefoucauld and the Art of the Self-Portrait." *Romanic Review* 65 (1974): 13–30.

———. "La Rochefoucauld et Jacques Esprit." *Revue d'Histoire Littéraire de la France* 78.2 (1978): 179–89.

Barthes, Roland. "La Rochefoucauld: 'Réflexions ou Sentences et Maximes.'" *"Le Degré zéro de l'écriture" suivi de "Nouveaux essais critiques."* 1953. Paris: Seuil, 1972. 69–88.

———. "Littérature et discontinu." *Essais critiques.* Paris: Seuil, 1964. 175–87.

———. *Nouveaux essais critiques.* Barthes, "La Rochefoucauld."

———. "Tacite et le baroque funèbre." *Essais critiques.* Paris: Seuil, 1964. 108–11.

Bazin, Jean de. *Index du vocabulaire des "Maximes" de La Rochefoucauld.* Paris: privately printed, 1967.

Beaujot, Jean-Pierre. "Le Travail de la définition dans quelques maximes de La Rochefoucauld." *Les Formes brèves de la prose et le discours discontinu (XVIᵉ et XVIIᵉ siècles).* Ed. J. Lafond. Paris: Vrin, 1984. 95–100.

Bénichou, Paul. "L'Intention des *Maximes.*" *L'Ecrivain et ses travaux.* Paris: Corti, 1967. 3–37.

———. *Morales du Grand Siècle.* Paris: Gallimard, 1948.

Benjamin, Walter. *The Origin of German Tragic Drama.* Trans. John Osborne. London: New Left Books (NLB), 1977.

———. *Ursprung des deutschen Trauerspiels.* Frankfurt: Suhrkamp, 1963.

Bigongiari, Piero. "Le 'Massime' di La Rochefoucauld." *La poesia come funzione simbolica del linguaggio.* Roma: Rizzoli Editore, 1972. 51–69.

Brody, Jules. "Les *Maximes* de La Rochefoucauld: Essai de lecture rhétorique." *Le Langage littéraire au XVIIᵉ siècle.* Ed. Christian Wentzlaff-Eggebert. Tübingen: Gunter Narr, 1991. 153–80.

Bruzzi, Amelia. *Dai "Mémoires" alle "Maximes" di La Rochefoucauld: La crisi di un moralista.* Bologna: R. Patron, 1965.

———. "Osservazioni sul linguaggio di un moralista: Appunti per un La Rochefoucauld barocco." *Il barocco nella poesia di Théophile de Viau.* Bologna: R. Patron, 1965. 143–69.

Burton, Robert. *The Anatomy of Melancholy.* Ed. T. C. Faulkner et al. 2 vols. Oxford: Clarendon, 1989.

Chamfort [Sébastien-Roch Nicolas]. *Maximes et pensées. Caractères et anecdotes.* Ed. Jean Dagen. Paris: Garnier–Flammarion, 1968.

Cioranescu, Alexandre. *Le Masque et le visage: Du baroque espagnol au classicisme français.* Genève: Droz, 1983.

Clark, Henry C. "La Rochefoucauld and the Social Bases of Aristocratic Ethics." *History of European Ideas* 8 (1987): 61–73.

Coulet, Henri. "La Rochefoucauld ou la peur d'être dupe." *Hommage au Doyen Etienne Gros.* Aix-en-Provence: Gap, 1959. 105–12.

Cuénin, Micheline. "Variation sur une maxime de La Rochefoucauld, le cœur dupé de l'esprit." *Mélanges Historiques et Littéraires sur le XVIIᵉ siècle.* Paris: Publications de la Société d'Etudes du XVIIᵉ siècle, 1974. 177–90.

Culler, Jonathan. "Paradox and the Language of Morals in La Rochefoucauld." *Modern Language Review* 68 (1973): 28–39.

Deleuze, Gilles. *Le Pli: Leibniz et le baroque.* Paris: Minuit, 1988.

Dens, Jean-Pierre. "Amour et amitié chez La Rochefoucauld." *Actes de Wake Forest.* Ed. M. Margitić and B. Wells. Paris-Seattle-Tübingen: PFSCL, 1987. 215–22.

———. "Morale et société chez La Rochefoucauld." *L'Information Littéraire* 28 (1975): 55–57.

Descartes, René. *Œuvres philosophiques.* Ed. Ferdinand Alquié. Paris: Garnier, 1973. Vol. 3.

Desfougères, Anne-Marie. "Des moralistes à la psychanalyse." *Destins et enjeux du XVIIᵉ siècle.* Ed. Yves-Marie Bercé. Paris: PUF, 1985. 241–51.

Donnellan, Brendan. "Nietzsche and La Rochefoucauld." *German Quarterly* 52 (1979): 303–18.

———. *Nietzsche and the French Moralists.* Bonn: Bouvier Verlag–Herbert Grundmann, 1982.

Doubrovsky, Serge. "Vingt propositions sur l'amour-propre: De Lacan à La Rochefoucauld." *Parcours critique.* Paris: Ed. Galilée, 1980. 203–34.

Dubois, Claude-Gilbert. *Le Baroque: Profondeurs de l'apparence.* Paris: Larousse, 1973.

Dyke, Daniel. *The Mystery of Selfe-deceiving; or, A Discourse and Discovery of the Deceitfulness of Mans Heart.* London: W. Stansby, 1634.

Encyclopédie ou dictionnaire raisonné des sciences, des arts et des métiers. Neufchastel: S. Faulche, 1765.

Faber, Marion. "The Metamorphosis of the French Aphorism: La Rochefoucauld and Nietzsche." *Comparative Literature Studies* 23.3 (1986): 205–17.

Fine, Peter Martin. *Vauvenargues and La Rochefoucauld.* Manchester: Manchester UP, 1974.

Freudmann, Felix R. "La Rochefoucauld and the Concept of Time." *Romance Notes* 3.2 (1962): 33–37.

Frey, Hans-Jost. "La Rochefoucauld und die Wahrheit." *Schweizer Monatshefte* 47 (1967): 388–94.

Furber, Donald. "The Myth of *Amour-propre* in La Rochefoucauld." *French Review* 43.2 (1969): 227–39.

Furetière, Antoine. *Dictionnaire universel.* Ed. Alain Rey. 3 vols. Paris: Le Robert, 1984.

Genette, Gérard. *Palimpsestes: La Littérature au second degré.* Paris: Seuil, 1982.

Giraldi, Giovanni. "Scettismo analitico di La Rochefoucauld." *Moralistica francese.* Milano: Edizione Pergamena, 1972. 85–118.

Gracián, Baltasar. *Obras completas.* Ed. Arturo del Hoyo. Madrid: Aguilar, 1960.

———. *The Oracle: A Manual of the Art of Discretion (Oráculo manual y arte de prudencia).* Trans. L. B. Walton. New York: William Salloch, 1953.

Granier, Jean. *Le Problème de la vérité dans la philosophie de Nietzsche.* Paris: Seuil, 1966.

Green, Robert. "Lost Paradise and Self-delusion in the Maxims of La Rochefoucauld." *French Review* 48.2 (1974): 321–30.

Hampton, Timothy. "Introduction: Baroques." "Baroque Topographies: Literature/History/Philosophy." Ed. Hampton. Special issue of *Yale French Studies* 80 (1991): 1–9.

Hayman, Ronald. *Nietzsche: A Critical Life.* London: Weidenfeld and Nicolson, 1980.

Hess, Gerhard. *Zur Entstehung der "Maximen" La Rochefoucaulds.* Köln: Westdeutscher Verlag, 1957.

Hippeau, Louis. *Essai sur la morale de La Rochefoucauld.* Paris: Nizet, 1967.

Hobbes, Thomas. *De Cive.* Ed. Howard Warrender. Oxford: Clarendon, 1983.

———. *Leviathan.* Ed. C. B. Macpherson. London: Penguin, 1968.

Hodgson, Richard G. "La Rochefoucauld and the Baroque Concept of *Inconstance.*" *Archiv für das Studium der neueren Sprachen und Literaturen* 228.2 (1991): 311–20.

Horowitz, Louise K. *Love and Language: A Study of the Classical French Moralist Writers.* Columbus: Ohio State UP, 1977. 29–49.

James, E. D. "Scepticism and Positive Values in La Rochefoucauld." *French Studies* 23 (1969): 349–61.

Jeanson, Francis. "Le Moraliste grandeur nature." *Lignes de départ.* Paris: Seuil, 1963. 71–107.

Krailsheimer, A. J. *Studies in Self-interest from Descartes to La Bruyère.* Oxford: Oxford UP, 1962.

Kruse, Margot. "La Rochefoucauld en Allemagne: Sa réception par Schopenhauer et Nietzsche." *Images de La Rochefoucauld: Actes du tricentenaire 1680–1980.* Ed. J. Lafond and J. Mesnard. Paris: PUF, 1984. 109–22.

———. *Die Maxime in der Französischen Literatur: Studien zum Werk La Rochefoucaulds und seiner Nachfolger.* Hamburg: Cram, De Gruyter, 1960.

La Bruyère, Jean de. *Les Caractères. Œuvres complètes.* Ed. Julien Benda. Bibliothèque de la Pléiade. Paris: Gallimard, 1951.

Lacan, Jacques. "Psychologie et métapsychologie." *Le Séminaire II: Le Moi dans la théorie de Freud et dans la technique de la psychanalyse.* Paris: Seuil, 1978.

———. "La Vérité surgit de la méprise." *Le Séminaire I: Les Ecrits techniques de Freud.* Ed. Jacques-Alain Miller. Paris: Seuil, 1975.

Lafond, Jean. "L'Amour-propre de La Rochefoucauld (MS 1). Histoire d'un thème et d'une forme." *Ouverture et dialogue: Mélanges offerts à Wolfgang Leiner.* Ed. Ulrich Doring et al. Tübingen: Gunter Narr, 1988. 263–76.

———. "Des formes brèves de la littérature morale aux XVIe et XVIIe siècles." *Les Formes brèves de la prose et le discours discontinu (XVIe et XVIIe siècles).* Ed. Lafond. Paris: Vrin, 1984. 101–22.

———. "Dit et non-dit dans les *Maximes.*" *Actes de Wake Forest.* Ed. M. Margitić and B. Wells. Paris-Seattle-Tübingen: PFSCL, 1987. 193–214.

———. "Dix ans d'étude sur les *Maximes* de La Rochefoucauld." *L'Information Littéraire* 39.1 (1987): 11–16.

———. *La Rochefoucauld: Augustinisme et littérature.* Paris: Klincksieck, 1977.

———. "La Rochefoucauld, d'une culture à l'autre." *Cahiers de l'Association Internationale des Etudes Françaises* 30 (1978): 155–69.

———. "La Rochefoucauld et les enjeux de l'écriture." *Papers on French Seventeenth Century Literature* 19 (1983): 711–31.

———. "La Rochefoucauld moraliste." *L'Information Littéraire* 28 (1976): 103–07.

167

Lafond, Jean. "Mentalité et discours de maîtrise, ou le moraliste en question." *Romanistische Zeitschrift für Literaturgeschichte* 3/4
(1988): 314–26.

———, ed. *Les Moralistes du XVIIe siècle.* Collection "Bouquins." Paris:
Laffont, 1992.

Laude, Patrick. "Perspectives on Subjectivity and the Ego in Seventeenth-
Century French Thought." *Papers on French Seventeenth Century Literature* 33 (1990): 531–46.

Lautréamont, comte de [Isidore Ducasse], and Germain Nouveau. *Œuvres
complètes.* Ed. Pierre-Olivier Walzer. Bibliothèque de la Pléiade.
Paris: Gallimard, 1970.

Leconte, Michelle. "Recherches sur les dates de composition des *Réflexions diverses* de La Rochefoucauld." *Revue des Sciences
Humaines* 118 (1965): 177–89.

Lerat, Pierre. "Le Distinguo dans les *Maximes* de La Rochefoucauld."
*Les Formes brèves de la prose et le discours discontinu (XVIe
et XVIIe siècles).* Ed. J. Lafond. Paris: Vrin, 1984. 91–94.

Levi, Anthony. *French Moralists: The Theory of the Passions, 1585 to
1649.* Oxford: Clarendon, 1964.

Lewis, Philip E. "La Rochefoucauld and the Rationality of Play." *Yale
French Studies* 41 (1968): 133–47.

———. *La Rochefoucauld: The Art of Abstraction.* Ithaca: Cornell UP, 1977.

Malebranche, Nicolas. *De la recherche de la vérité.* Ed. G. Rodis-Lewis.
2 vols. Paris: Vrin, 1945.

Manzon, Jean. *Réflexions et maximes morales de M. le Duc de la
Rochefoucault.* Amsterdam: J. G. Baerstecher, 1772.

Martin, Paul. "La Paresse béatifique: Etude d'une maxime de La
Rochefoucauld." *L'Information Littéraire* 35 (1983): 115–24.

Mathieu-Castellani, Gisèle. "Discours maniériste, discours baroque:
Narcisse et Pygmalion." *Du Baroque aux lumières: Pages à
la mémoire de Jeanne Carriat.* Paris: Rougerie, 1986. 21–23.

McBride, Robert. "The Triumph of Art over Nature in the *Maximes.*"
Aspects of Seventeenth-Century Drama and Thought. London:
Macmillan, 1979. 90–111.

Meleuc, Serge. "Structure de la maxime." *Langages* 13 (1969): 69–99.

Mercanton, Jacques. "La Rochefoucauld: Un Style et une vision." *Le
Siècle des grandes ombres.* Vevey: Editions Bertil Galland,
1981. 55–73.

Méré, chevalier de. *Œuvres complètes.* Ed. Charles-H. Boudhors. 3 vols.
Paris: Editions Fernand Roches, 1930.

Mesnard, Jean. "L'Esthétique de La Rochefoucauld." *Actes de Wake Forest.* Ed. M. Margitić and B. Wells. Paris-Seattle-Tübingen: PFSCL, 1987. 235–50.

Montaigne, Michel de. *Œuvres complètes.* Ed. A. Thibaudet and M. Rat. Bibliothèque de la Pléiade. Paris: Gallimard, 1962.

Montandon, Alain. *Les Formes brèves.* Collection "Contours littéraires." Paris: Hachette, 1992.

Moore, W. G. *La Rochefoucauld, His Mind and Art.* Oxford: Clarendon, 1969.

———. "La Rochefoucauld's Masterpiece." *Linguistic and Literary Studies in Honor of H. A. Hatzfeld.* Washington, DC: Catholic U of America P, 1964. 263–68.

———. "The World of La Rochefoucauld's *Maximes.*" *French Studies* 7 (1953): 325–45.

Mora, Edith. *François de La Rochefoucauld.* Paris: Seghers, 1965.

Morel, Jacques. "Les *Maximes* et le théâtre." *L'Intelligence du passé, les faits, l'écriture et le sens: Mélanges offerts à Jean Lafond par ses amis.* Ed. P. Aquilon, J. Chupeau, and F. Weil. Tours: Université de Tours, 1988. 475–80.

Morello, André-Alain. "Actualité de La Rochefoucauld." *Moralistes du XVIIe siècle.* Ed. Jean Lafond. Collection "Bouquins." Paris: Laffont, 1992. 103–28.

Moriarty, Michael. "La Rochefoucauld: Tastes and Their Vicissitudes." *Taste and Ideology in Seventeenth-Century France.* Cambridge: Cambridge UP, 1988. 120–40.

Mourgues, Odette de. *Two French Moralists: La Rochefoucauld and La Bruyère.* Cambridge: Cambridge UP, 1978.

Nemer, Monique. "Les Intermittences de la vérité: Maxime, sentence ou aphorisme: Notes sur l'évolution d'un genre." *Studi Francesi* 26 (1982): 484–93.

Nicole, Pierre. *Essais de morale.* 3 vols. Genève: Slatkine, 1971.

Nietzsche, Friedrich. *Daybreak: Thoughts on the Prejudices of Morality.* Trans. R. J. Hollingdale. Cambridge: Cambridge UP, 1982.

———. *Human, All Too Human: A Book for Free Spirits.* Trans. R. J. Hollingdale. Cambridge: Cambridge UP, 1986.

———. "On Truth and Lies in a Normal Sense." Nietzsche, *Philosophy and Truth.*

———. *Philosophy and Truth: Selections from Nietzsche's Notebooks of the Early 1870's.* Trans. and ed. Daniel Breazeale. Atlantic Highlands, NJ: Humanities, 1979.

169

Nietzsche, Friedrich. *Werke.* 21 vols. New York-Berlin: Walter de Gruyter, 1968–77.

Pascal, Blaise. *Pensées.* Ed. Philippe Sellier. Paris: Mercure de France, 1976.

Poulet, Georges. *La Pensée indéterminée: I. De la renaissance au romantisme.* Paris: PUF, 1985. 82–86.

Richelet, Pierre. *Dictionnaire françois.* 2 vols. Genève: Slatkine, 1970.

Rohou, Jean. "L'Amour de soi au XVIIᵉ siècle: De la concupiscence à la complaisance, à l'angoisse et à l'intérêt." *Les Visages de l'amour au XVIIᵉ siècle.* Université de Toulouse–Le Mirail: Service des Publications, 1984. 79–89.

Rosso, Corrado. "Démarches et structures de compensation dans les Maximes de La Rochefoucauld." *Cahiers de l'Association Internationale des Etudes Françaises* 18 (1966): 113–24.

———. *Procès à La Rochefoucauld.* Paris: Nizet, 1986.

———. "Une Rencontre devant les rayons d'une bibliothèque: La Rochefoucauld et Marx." *Ouverture et dialogue: Mélanges offerts à Wolfgang Leiner.* Tübingen: Gunter Narr, 1988. 349–56.

———. *Virtu et critica della virtu nei moralisti francesi: La Rochefoucauld, La Bruyère, Vauvenargues.* 1964. Pisa: Editrice Libreria Goliardica, 1971.

Rostand, Jean. "La Rochefoucauld." *Hommes de vérité.* Paris: Stock,1942. 19–44.

Roth, Oskar. "La Rochefoucauld: Das Wertbewusstsein eines Frondeurs." *Romanistische Zeitschrift für Literaturgeschichte* 1 (1977): 491–513.

Rousset, Jean. *L'Intérieur et l'extérieur: Essai sur la poésie et sur le théâtre au XVIIᵉ siècle.* Paris: Corti, 1976.

———. *La Littérature de l'âge baroque en France.* Paris: Corti, 1954.

———. "La Rochefoucauld contre le classicisme." *Archiv für das Studium der neueren Sprachen und Literaturen* 179–81 (1941–42): 107–12.

Sainte-Beuve, Charles Augustin. *Portraits de femmes. Œuvres.* Ed. Maxime Leroy. Bibliothèque de la Pléiade. Paris: Gallimard, 1961.

Scarpetta, Guy. *L'Artifice.* Paris: Grasset, 1988.

Schabert, Tilo. "The Para-moral Principles of Early Modern Society: Contextual Reflections upon the Maxims of La Rochefoucauld." *History of European Ideas* 7 (1986): 67–84.

Sellier, Philippe. "La Rochefoucauld, Pascal, Saint-Augustin." *Revue d'Histoire Littéraire de la France* 69.3–4 (1969): 551–75.

Souiller, Didier. *La Littérature baroque en Europe.* Paris: PUF, 1986.

Stackelberg, Jürgen von. *Französische Moralistik im europäischen Kontext.* Darmstadt: Wissenschaftliche Buchgesellschaft, 1982.

Stanton, Domna C. *The Aristocrat as Art: A Study of the Honnête Homme and the Dandy in Seventeenth- and Nineteenth-Century French Literature.* New York: Columbia UP, 1980.

Starobinski, Jean. "Complexité de La Rochefoucauld." *Preuves* 135 (1962): 33–40.

———. "La Rochefoucauld ou l'oubli des secrets." *Médecine de la France* 107 (1959): 34–40.

———. *Montaigne en mouvement.* Paris: Gallimard, 1982.

Steland, Dieter. *Moralistik und Erzählkunst von La Rochefoucauld und Mme de Lafayette bis Marivaux.* München: W. Fink, 1985.

Sutcliffe, F. E. "The System of La Rochefoucauld." *Bulletin of the John Rylands Library* 49 (1966): 233–45.

Thweatt, Vivien. *La Rochefoucauld and the Seventeenth-Century Concept of the Self.* Genève: Droz, 1980.

Tiefenbrun, Susan W. "Wit, beyond Freud, and the *Maxims* of La Rochefoucauld." *Papers on French Seventeenth Century Literature* 33 (1980): 239–83.

Todorov, Tzvetan. "La Comédie humaine selon La Rochefoucauld." *Poétique* 53 (1983): 37–47.

Toner, Fred. "La Question de l'utilité dans les *Maximes* de La Rochefoucauld." *Chimères* 16.2 (1983): 19–34.

Van Delft, Louis. "La Rochefoucauld, moraliste mondain." *Studi Francesi* 72 (1980): 415–25.

———. "Lieux d'échanges, lieux communs: L'Espace de la réflexion morale." *Horizons Européens de la Littérature Française au XVIIᵉ Siècle.* Ed. Wolfgang Leiner. Tübingen: Gunter Narr Verlag, 1988. 267–76.

———. *Le Moraliste classique.* Genève: Droz, 1982.

———. "Pour une lecture mondaine de La Rochefoucauld." *Images de La Rochefoucauld.* Ed. J. Lafond et J. Mesnard. Paris: PUF, 1984.

———. "La Spécificité du moraliste classique." *Revue d'Histoire Littéraire de la France* 80 (1980): 540–53.

Vauvenargues, Luc de Clapiers, marquis de. *Œuvres complètes.* Ed. Henry Bonnier. 2 vols. Paris: Hachette, 1968.

Wagner, N. "De la méthode dans les *Maximes* de La Rochefoucauld." *L'Information Littéraire* 3 (1955): 89–100.

Weber, Joseph G. "The *Maximes* as Theater." *Actes de Wake Forest*. Ed. M. Margitić and B. Wells. Paris-Seattle-Tübingen: PFSCL, 1987. 223–34.

⸻. "The Personae in the Style of La Rochefoucauld's *Maximes*." *PMLA* 89 (1974): 250–55.

Westgate, Donald. "The Concept of *Amour-propre* in the *Maximes* of La Rochefoucauld." *Nottingham French Studies* 7.2 (1968): 67–79.

Zeller, Mary Francine. *New Aspects of Style in the "Maximes" of La Rochefoucauld*. Washington, DC: Catholic U of America P, 1954.

Index